Literacy World

Stage 4 Non-Fiction Literacy Lesso
Teacher's Guide

Welcome to Literacy World!

What is Literacy World?

Literacy World is a complete literacy programme for 7–11 year olds. It is structured around the format of the Literacy Hour, and linked closely to the teaching objectives contained in the National Literacy Strategy *Framework for teaching*. Because it is fundamentally a balanced literacy programme, schools not implementing the NLS *Framework* can also use it.

Literacy World consists of two strands, covering fiction and non-fiction. This *Literacy Lesson Teacher's Guide* is designed to help you to teach the non-fiction strand of *Literacy World*.

Literacy World non-fiction components

There are four stages in *Literacy World* non-fiction: Stage 1 for Year 3, Stage 2 for Year 4, Stage 3 for Year 5 and Stage 4 for Year 6. Each stage consists of the following components:

Literacy Lesson Teacher's Guide

The *Literacy Lesson Teacher's Guides* provide weekly lesson plans structured around the Literacy Hour. They give guidance on the features of each of the non-fiction text types and structured lessons on how to introduce them to children. This leads into developing children's writing of non-fiction in a supportive way. The *Teacher's Guides* also provide suggestions and photocopiable material for follow-up and group work.

Pages 4 and 5 of this guide explain in more detail how to use the *Literacy Lesson Teacher's Guides*.

Literacy Skills Big Books

There are two *Literacy Skills Big Books* for each stage. These books are designed to be used alongside the lesson plans in the *Literacy Lesson Teacher's Guides*. The big books contain model texts of each of the main text types (reports, recounts, instructional texts, etc.) to help you to introduce the key features of the text types to the children, followed by extracts from the pupil books. The books focus on the skills required to read and write the different non-fiction text types at text, sentence and word level (e.g. skimming for information, use of charts and diagrams, headings, understanding the structure of non-fiction text types).

Information Books

The *Literacy World* information books introduce children to all the non-fiction text types covered in the National Literacy Strategy *Framework for teaching*. They are ideal for Guided Reading and other extension work in groups. As well as matching the text type requirements, they also progressively introduce a wide variety of non-fiction features. The books are designed to reflect children's interests and cover topics which are relevant to other areas of the curriculum.

Reference Texts

There are four reference texts in the *Literacy World* non-fiction strand: a dictionary and an encyclopedia for Stages 1 and 2, and another dictionary and encyclopedia for Stages 3 and 4. These books come in both small and big versions, and are designed to help you to deliver the NLS objectives for using reference texts.

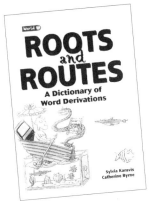

Guided Reading Cards

There is a set of Guided Reading Cards to complement the information books and reference texts at each stage. These cards provide suggestions for Guided Reading activities using the *Literacy World* books. Each card is two-sided, with teacher-led activities on one side and suggestions for independent group work on the reverse.

How to use Literacy World non-fiction in the classroom

The information books and reference texts in *Literacy World* are designed to be used in a number of ways:

Each book should be introduced to children during a Shared Reading session. Extracts from the information books have been reproduced in large format in the *Literacy Skills Big Books*, and the reference texts are also available in big book form for this purpose. The lesson plans in the *Non-Fiction Literacy Lesson Teacher's Guides* are designed to help you use the big books to:

→ show the children how to read and **use** non-fiction books effectively through modelling reading strategies (e.g. skimming, making notes from text);

→ teach the children the **features** of non-fiction books (e.g. headings, captions);

→ introduce non-fiction **text types** to the children (e.g. report, explanation);

→ teach the **language features** common to the different text types (e.g. the use of the past tense in recounts).

After the children have been introduced to the books during a Shared Reading session, the information books and reference texts can be further explored during Guided Reading, when the skills needed to use the books effectively can be reinforced. Guided Reading Cards have been provided to help you to structure these sessions.

The books can also be used independently in further group work as models for the children's own non-fiction writing.

How to use the Literacy Lesson Teacher's Guides

The weekly lesson plans are the heart of the *Literacy Lesson Teacher's Guides*. Each lesson is divided into whole class shared reading/writing, group activities and plenary sessions.

Each unit consists of two weeks' Literacy Hour teaching based around one Literacy World information book (or one week's teaching for each reference text).

The teaching objectives for each lesson relate directly to the NLS termly text, sentence and word level objectives.

Lessons link directly to the extracts in the Literacy Skills Big Books.

Unit 1

Alan Shearer: A Biography

Text type: Recount/Biography

Learning Outcomes:

To become familiar with the content, structure and language features typical of biographical writing; to distinguish between biographical and autobiographical writing.

Preparation:

Collect examples of biographical and autobiographical writing. Include in the collection 'fanzines', theatre and football programmes and other publications that contain biographical information.

The written outcome of this unit is individual biographies written by the children. They could all write about the same person, a person of their own choice, a friend or member of their family. You may wish to tie this in with another curriculum area and ask the children to write a biography of a scientist, explorer or inventor.

Show the class the book you are going to study. Explain that you are going to work with enlarged pages from *Alan Shearer: A Biography* to ensure that everyone can see clearly.

Lesson 1

Spotlight on: Immersion

Teaching Objective

- *To distinguish between biography and autobiography (Y6 T1 T11)*

Whole Class Shared Reading

Mask the words *A Biography* on the front cover of the *Alan Shearer: A Biography* big book. Read the title of the book and ask the children what sort of information they would expect to find in the book and who might have written it. List the children's responses.

Look through the book, drawing attention to the headings. Do they help to confirm the children's predictions? Read pages 4 and 5. Ask whether the children think this was written by Alan Shearer. Reveal the rest of the cover title and discuss the terms *biography* and *autobiography*. You may wish to refer to a dictionary to explore the definitions of the

two prefixes. Remind the children of the introduction they read on pages 4 and 5, and the fact that it was written in the third person. Discuss how it would differ if it was written in the first person.

Group Activities

- In pairs, the children can sort through the collection of biographical and autobiographical writing and identify which is which.
- The children can complete PCM 3 (see page 22).

Plenary

Ask several children to report on their findings. Did they have any difficulty in classifying the writing?

The children can give examples with meanings from their completed PCM.

Lesson 2

Spotlight on: Immersion

Teaching Objective

- *To distinguish between biography and autobiography (Y6 T1 T11)*

Whole Class Shared Reading

Ask the children to think about the similarities between biographies and autobiographies. Remind them that, while both are likely to record events, an autobiography is likely to contain incidents, thoughts and feelings known only to the author. A biography includes comments made by others about the subject and is unable to include personal details unless the subject has made them known.

Explain that you are going to look for comments made about Alan Shearer by others. Skim through the pages of the big book to find examples of quotes. Read the quotations and note down some of the words used to describe Shearer. Discuss with the children what they feel they now know about Shearer. Is it fact or opinion?

Group Activities

Individually or in pairs, the children can select words from those noted in the whole class session and define them using General PCM 3 (see page 72).

Plenary

Ask a few children to read out their own definitions. Challenge the rest of the class to decide on their accuracy before reading the dictionary definition.

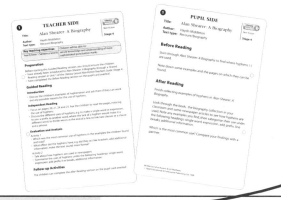

The lessons all include suggestions for children's independent group work. Ideas for teacher-led Guided Reading sessions can be found separately in the Guided Reading Cards provided for each book.

Lesson ❸

Spotlight on: Discovery

Teaching Objective

- To distinguish between biography and autobiography (Y6 T1 T11)

Whole Class Shared Reading

Read the model text on pages 2 and 3 of the big book. Focus on the use of paragraphs. Discuss with the children the main points of each paragraph and write these on the acetate sheet. Discuss the purpose of the text with the children.

Group Activities

Using examples from the collection of biographical and autobiographical writing, ask the children to do a similar analysis of textual organisation.

Plenary

Using the feedback from the children, draw up a framework for a biography. You may wish to use PCM 1 as a model. Use the feedback from the children to reinforce the differences and similarities between recounts and biographies.

Lesson ❹

Spotlight on: Discovery

Teaching Objective

- To distinguish between biography and autobiography (Y6 T1 T11)

Whole Class Shared Reading

Before reading, discuss with the children the use of tables and grids to present information, e.g. their purposes, when they are used and which text types are likely to contain them. Look through the pages of the big book and briefly look at and discuss the different tables and grids and the information they give. Discuss how they can contribute to clarity and how complicated or lengthy details can be summarised for the reader to understand at a glance.

Turn to page 9 and read the information in the table. Discuss with the children how the information could be given solely using text. Focus particularly on the map, drawings of the strip and the club badge.

Using the acetate sheet, demonstrate how to highlight key words and phrases on page 8.

Group Activities

The children can complete PCM 4 (see page 23) to summarise and represent detailed information.

Plenary

Ask some children to read out their fact panels. Do other children agree with their analyses? Were there any discrepancies? If so what were they and why were these areas problematic? You may wish to use the feedback to draw up a revision poster on how to extract information.

Lesson ❺

Spotlight on: Familiarisation

Teaching Objectives

- To distinguish between biography and autobiography (Y6 T1 T11)
- To revise word classes, re-expressing sentences, complex sentences, standard English, adapting texts (Y6 T1 S1)
- To form complex sentences (Y6 T1 S5)

Whole Class Shared Reading

Using the model text on pages 2 and 3 of the big book, highlight the language features typical of a biography. Use the annotated version on pages 14 and 15 of this guide to ensure that all the relevant features are covered.

Remind the children of the difference between biography and autobiography and the uses of the 1st and 3rd person. Ensure that children understand the difference between the two voices.

Focus on the connecting words and phrases found in this text and their effect.

Read pages 10 and 11 and ask the children to listen for words and phrases that connect events or ideas. List their suggestions.

Group Activities

- The children can find and list further examples in other biographical texts.
- They can complete PCM 2 (see page 21).
- Some children may extend this to looking for connecting words and phrases in other text types.

Plenary

Ask the children to report on their findings. Add further words and phrases to the chart.

PCMs are designed to provide a focus for group activities. The Teacher's Guides also include a number of general PCMs (pages 70–77) linked to the lessons and the Guided Reading Cards. Some of these PCMs can also be used as part of continuous assessment.

The lesson plans give detailed guidance on how to use the model texts in the big books to help the children to understand the structure and features of the different text types, and to help to construct a writing framework for each type.

Annotated versions of the model texts are provided in the Teacher's Guide.

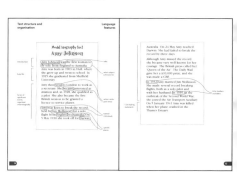

17

A model of literacy teaching

The model of literacy teaching used in the *Non-Fiction Literacy World Teacher's Guides* is one that is increasingly used to support children's learning. It draws on the work of teachers and researchers such as Lunzer and Gardner, Derewianka, Christie, Martin and Rothery, Lewis and Wray and many others. In particular, it recognises that effective literacy teaching exploits the links between reading and writing.

The model takes account of the fact that, when faced with the challenge of learning something new, a learner needs to review existing knowledge and be supported in becoming familiar with and analysing new information, in order to assimilate new knowledge and apply it independently.

The role of the teacher in this model is to:
- make explicit what is to be learned;
- scaffold the learning process;
- help children to review their learning.

The teaching strategies and groupings described in the *Non-Fiction Literacy Lesson Teacher's Guides* reflect those described in the NLS *Framework for teaching*.

Stages in the model – making the links between reading and writing

It is assumed that children will experience the reading and writing of non-fiction texts in a variety of contexts and in as many forms as possible, including IT.

Immersion

The teacher and the children collect, read and discuss examples of the text type being studied.

Discovery

The teacher helps the children to read and identify significant organisational features of the text and supports the children in developing a framework for the text type.

Familiarisation

The teacher provides opportunities for the children to become familiar with the text structure, organisation and language features of the text.

The writing process

Shared writing

The teacher models the writing process using the previously developed framework. The children, where necessary, use writing frames to structure their writing. It should be noted that writing frames are not in themselves a purpose for writing. They should only be used to provide a structure for organising texts for those children who need them.

Independent writing

The children, in pairs or individually, apply their knowledge to plan and draft a similarly structured text.

At all stages, the teacher helps the children to question and clarify their learning by providing opportunities for reflection and discussion. The way that this model works in practice is made clear in the lesson plans for each book.

You may find it helpful to develop reference posters with the children defining some of the technical terms used to describe aspects of non-fiction texts. As you focus on a particular text type it is worthwhile producing an ongoing working wall display where frameworks, lists of typical language features, examples of shared writing, children's drafts and published writing illustrate the reading to writing process and provide a rich resource for the children to refer to. Suggestions of work to add to the wall charts can be found in the lesson plans.

Assessment

Assessing reading

Teachers use a variety of contexts and methods to assess children's reading, ranging from individual reading conferences to standardised reading tests. The Guided Reading and Plenary sessions in the Literacy Hour can provide further opportunities for collecting useful information about children's reading. For example, the explicit attention given to reading strategies during Shared Reading can be observed, discussed and noted by the teacher during a Guided Reading session. Plenary sessions, where children reflect on their learning, can be used to focus their attention on their own reading. These reflections can provide the teacher with valuable assessment information.

The children themselves should also be actively involved in assessing themselves as readers. If children are to be successful, they need to know what is expected of them and how to achieve it. They should have opportunities to reflect on themselves as readers and the strategies they use, to identify successes and areas where they still need practice or help. General PCM 7 (see page 76 of this guide) is provided to help children make judgements about their own reading.

When reading non-fiction the literate primary child:
- is able to use contents and index and can explain the differences between them;
- knows a text can be accessed through a variety of signposts, e.g. headings, illustrations, bullet points, asterisks;
- knows the purposes of different types of illustrations and can explain why they are used, e.g. charts, maps, diagrams;
- applies and can explain a range of strategies used to read, e.g. skim for overall effect, scan to locate specific information, close read to enquire further;
- can review existing knowledge and formulate research questions;
- reads with a definite purpose in mind, e.g. to find an answer to a particular question, to follow up personal interests;
- is able to locate and use relevant information;
- can make judgements about the text being read, e.g. accuracy of information, presentation;
- can analyse the structure of a text, e.g. introduction, main sections, summary;
- can identify topic sentences and main ideas in paragraphs;
- can evaluate the effectiveness of non-fiction texts and give reasons for judgements;
- can compare non-fiction texts on the same subject;
- can use appropriate terminology when talking about non-fiction;
- is aware of authors' intentions or bias;
- can identify a range of text types.

Assessing writing

When assessing writing, it is important to make a balanced assessment that includes judgements about content, organisation, language and secretarial features. When responding to a piece of writing, children can be helped to see how improvements may be made if comments are organised under separate headings for content and organisation and secretarial aspects. This separation of composition from the surface features of writing helps developing writers to understand that meaning and clarity are at least as important as spelling and handwriting.

As with reading, children should be involved in making judgements about their own writing. General PCM 8 (see page 77 of this guide) could be used as a means of encouraging children to reflect on and check through a piece of writing. This process promotes reflection and emphasises the responsibilities of a writer towards a reader. The completed PCM could then be attached to the draft or final piece *before* the teacher responds.

When writing non-fiction the literate primary child:
- knows the structure and features of a range of non-fiction text types;
- selects the appropriate text type for purpose and intended audience;
- uses language appropriate to the chosen text type;
- selects an effective means of conveying information to a reader, e.g. diagram, graph, table;
- knows how to integrate text and illustrations to enhance meaning and aid the reader;
- can make notes from a text using key words and phrases;
- can organise notes to plan and write coherently;
- draws on research notes and prior knowledge to plan and draft;
- can apply editing techniques to improve the text;
- can proof read to produce a final draft;
- can use font and typeface appropriate to purpose and audience.

Year 6 NLS correlation chart

The *Literacy World* Year 6 non-fiction texts and related lessons cover most of the NLS non-fiction reading and writing text level objectives, and also some word and sentence level objectives where these arise naturally from the books. This chart lists all the objectives covered.

	Unit 1 — Alan Shearer: A Biography	Unit 2 — Spiders (and how they hunt)	Unit 3 — Big Issues	Unit 4 — Quakes, Floods and Other Disasters	Unit 5 — An Encyclopedia of Myths and Legends	Unit 6 — Roots and Routes: A Dictionary of Word Derivations
Term 1 — Text level						
11 to distinguish between biography and autobiography	✓					
13 to secure understanding of the features of reports		✓				
14 to develop the skills of biographical and autobiographical writing	✓					
15 to develop a journalistic style		✓				
16 to use the styles and conventions of journalism to report on events		✓				
17 to write non-chronological reports linked to other subjects		✓				
18 to use IT to bring writing to publication standard		✓				
Sentence level						
1 to revise word classes, re-expressing sentences, complex sentences, standard English, adapting texts	✓					
5 to form complex sentences	✓	✓				
Term 2 — Text level						
15 to recognise how arguments are constructed to be effective			✓			
16 to identify the features of balanced written arguments			✓			
18 to construct effective arguments			✓			
Sentence level						
2 to understand features of formal official language			✓			
5 to use reading to investigate conditionals			✓			
Word level						
8 to build a bank of useful terms and phrases for argument			✓			

Text level

	Unit 1	Unit 2	Unit 3	Unit 4	Unit 5	Unit 6
15 to secure understanding of the key features of explanatory texts				✓		
16 to identify the key features of impersonal formal language				✓		
17 to appraise a text quickly and effectively; to find information quickly				✓		✓
18 to secure the skills of skimming, scanning and efficient reading				✓		
19 to review a range of non-fiction text types and their characteristics				✓	✓	
20 to secure control of impersonal writing				✓		
22 to select the appropriate style and form to suit purpose and audience				✓	✓	✓

Sentence level

	Unit 1	Unit 2	Unit 3	Unit 4	Unit 5	Unit 6
1 to revise the language and grammatical features of the text types				✓		
2 to conduct detailed language investigations					✓	
3 to revise formal styles of writing				✓		
4 to secure control of complex sentences				✓		

Word level

	Unit 1	Unit 2	Unit 3	Unit 4	Unit 5	Unit 6
2 to use known spellings as a basis for spelling other words						✓
5 to invent words using known roots, prefixes and suffixes						✓
6 to practise and extend vocabulary					✓	✓
7 to experiment with language					✓	✓

Year 6 non-fiction features chart

Structure and layout

	Alan Shearer: A Biography	Spiders (and how they hunt)	Big Issues	Quakes, Floods and Other Disasters	Encyclopedia of Myths and Legends	Roots and Routes: A Dictionary of Word Derivations
Cover	✓	✓	✓	✓	✓	✓
Contents page	✓	✓	✓	✓		✓
Index	✓	✓	✓	✓	✓	
Glossary		✓			✓	
Bibliography		✓	✓			✓
Headings and sub-headings	✓	✓	✓	✓	✓	✓
Paragraphs	✓	✓	✓	✓		
Bulleted lists		✓	✓	✓		
Captions	✓	✓	✓	✓		

Visual information

	Alan Shearer: A Biography	Spiders (and how they hunt)	Big Issues	Quakes, Floods and Other Disasters	Encyclopedia of Myths and Legends	Roots and Routes: A Dictionary of Word Derivations
Diagrams: labelled		✓		✓		
cross-section		✓		✓		
cut-away				✓		
Graphs			✓			
Tables	✓	✓	✓	✓		
Maps	✓			✓	✓	✓
Timelines						✓
Flow charts		✓				

Literacy World and the Scottish 5 – 14 Guidelines

The following chart shows where, in Stages 3 and 4 of *Literacy World* non-fiction, you can find the most appropriate components for meeting the Level D and E Attainment Targets (ATs). The reading and writing strands of the Scottish Guidelines are interwoven throughout the fiction and non-fiction teaching units in *Literacy World*. *Literacy World* non-fiction takes as its starting point the teaching of genre through examples in the *Literacy Skills Big Book*s. From this starting point the features of non-fiction books and the skills associated with using them are taught. Specific grammar and vocabulary work is also taught from the *Big Books*. To find where each genre is taught, refer to the contents page on page 1 of this guide. To find where specific organisational and language features, grammatical terms and spelling and vocabulary skills are taught, refer to the NLS correlation charts on pages 8 and 9 of this guide.

Writing strand	Level D	Level E	Components in *Literacy World* non-fiction
Functional writing	Write in a variety of forms to communicate key events, facts or ideas, using appropriate organisation and vocabulary.	Write in a variety of forms to communicate key events, facts, points of view and ideas, using appropriate organisation and vocabulary.	Photocopiable writing frames in the *Non-Fiction Literacy Lesson Teacher's Guides* help support children's functional writing.
Personal writing	Write about personal experiences, expressing thoughts and feelings for a specific purpose and audience and using appropriate organisation and vocabulary.	Write about personal experiences in a variety of formats, demonstrating some capacity to reflect on experience with some grasp of appropriate style.	Practice in writing personal recounts can be found in the lesson plans and PCMs in the *Teacher's Guides*.
Punctuation and structure	In the writing tasks above, punctuate most sentences accurately; achieve some variety in sentence structure; use paragraphs; and begin to indicate speech in some way where appropriate.	In the writing tasks above, construct, punctuate and link sentences of different lengths, and organised them in paragraphs in order to shape meaning.	Punctuation and structure are developed throughout the lesson plans. Within the teaching of non-fiction, the use of connectives is a strong feature.
Knowledge about language	Show that they know, understand and can use at least the following terms: vowel and consonant, adjective, adverb, pronoun and conjunction; masculine and feminine, singular and plural; tense; paragraph.	Show that they know, understand and can use the following terms: main point, topic sentence, evidence; subject, predicate, clause; quotation marks, apostrophe; punctuation.	The chart on pages 8 and 9 of this guide gives a detailed breakdown of the language features covered in *Literacy World* non-fiction. Planning and drafting is strongly developed in the Shared Writing strand of the lesson plans.

Reading strand	Level D	Level E	Components in *Literacy World* non-fiction
Reading for information	Find, select and collate information from more than one source.	Apply the information acquired from a number of different sources for the purposes of a piece of personal research.	All the non-fiction information books at Stages 3 and 4; teacher-led modelling of these skills through the *Literacy Skills Big Books* and the *Teacher's Guides*.
Awareness of genre	Identify some similarities and differences of form and content in examples of the same type of text, for example ghost stories or letters of complaint or short biographical terms from an encyclopedia.	Identify some similarities and differences of form and content in examples of texts from a variety of genres, and comment on how these reflect the texts' purposes.	The non-fiction books have been written as models of genre. In addition, the *Teacher's Guide* introduces each genre with a model text, with full guidance on how to teach it.
Knowledge about language	Show that they know, understand and can use at least the following terms: theme, character, relationships, setting, motives; fact and opinion; layout, bold and italic type.	Show that they know, understand and can use the following terms: genre; syllable, root, stem, prefix, suffix; simile, metaphor.	The chart on pages 8 and 9 of this guide gives a detailed breakdown of the language features covered in *Literacy World* non-fiction.

Literacy World and the Northern Ireland Curriculum

The following chart shows how *Literacy World* non-fiction meets the programme of study for Key Stage 2 English in Northern Ireland. The Speaking and Listening Attainment Target has not been specifically included on this chart, but *Literacy World* encourages oral communication in its Shared and Guided Reading components.

Reading

Context and Audience: The Guided Reading strand of *Literacy World* offers opportunities for reading individually, to the teacher and in groups or pairs. The Shared Reading strand, based on the *Non-Fiction Literacy Skills Big Books*, is designed for whole class reading.

Range: *Literacy World* non-fiction offers a whole range of non-fiction texts, including dictionaries and encyclopedias.

Purpose: *Literacy World* encourages independent reading for information and enjoyment. The non-fiction books are designed to teach the skills required to read and use non-fiction, including locating information. They are also designed to be used in other areas of the curriculum.

Activities: The Shared Reading lesson plans and Guided Reading Cards offer strategies for helping children understand texts. They focus on distinctive features of a text, encourage reading aloud, contain activities on representing texts in different visual forms, and consistently encourage personal responses to the texts. They also look at how meaning can be manipulated through language. Texts are revisited after initial reading, encouraging children to review initial response. Features of language are comprehensively covered in the lesson plans and the *Literacy Skills Big Books*.

Expected Outcomes: The Shared Reading lesson plans and the Guided Reading Cards encourage sensitive response to texts, and writers' intentions are discussed. They demand use of organisational information, deal with how different media present information and teach understanding of different reading skills. There are many opportunities for children to model their own writing on texts read and to write for different audiences.

Writing

Planning: Planning is encouraged in the Shared Reading lesson plans, modelled by the teacher in the *Big Books* and supported by PCMs. It includes discussion, gathering and organising ideas, making notes and preparing outlines.

Purpose: The Shared Reading lesson plans require the children to develop their skills in reporting, informing, explaining, persuading, interpreting data and giving instructions.

Context and Audience: Writing arises mainly from responses to reading. Children are encouraged to consider audience in their writing and specific work is done on adapting texts for different audiences.

Range: *Literacy World* non-fiction includes the writing of reports, instructions, letters and notes, as well as discussions about layout and use of the alphabet. The differences between spoken and written language are revisited throughout the scheme in different contexts.

Expected Outcomes: The lesson plans for all of the non-fiction books look at presenting and structuring information and opinions, and observing the different conventions and structures demanded by different text types. Grammar and punctuation are also taught where they arise naturally from the books.

Year 6: Unit 1

Recount/Biography: *Alan Shearer: A Biography*

Introduction

Most children will have had some experience of biographical information in both written and visual forms. Consequently, they are likely to have an implicit understanding of the kind of information contained in this text type although they may not necessarily understand explicitly the structure and organisation.

A biography is an account of one person's life written by another person. It has many of the features of a recount. In addition, because biographies feature a specific subject and are, on the whole, written in a narrative style, it may sometimes appear to be a story. To complicate matters further, by using information gleaned through reading a novel, it is possible to produce a biography of a fictional character. The fact that biographical writing can be used in fictional contexts can cause children problems when approaching this text type.

Biographies fall within the range of non-fiction text types. They contain details of the subject's life, such as events and dates, that can be checked for accuracy. Along with verifiable information, biographies often include other people's views of the subject or events the subject was involved in. Whilst these may be accurate in terms of dates and specific events, the way in which the contributor gives the information is from a personal perspective. It is the mixture of fact and opinion that makes biographies interesting and challenging.

Alan Shearer: A Biography contains many of the features typical of a biography, including dates, events, photographs and quotes from other people. Each double page spread gives precise information together with background details about significant events in Shearer's life and career.

On pages 2 and 3 of the big book you will find a model biography. This has been specially written to contain the structural and linguistic features typical of a biography. We suggest that you go through this model text with the children, pointing out the typical features of the text type. The sheet of acetate provided with the big books is designed to be placed in front of the model texts so that you can write your own notes and annotations around the text. Further information on using the model text can be found in the notes for Lesson 5, and on pages 14 and 15 of this guide you will find an annotated version of the same text to help you to draw out its relevant features.

At the end of this unit you may wish to use General PCMs 2, 5, 7 and 8 as part of continuous assessment.

Structural and linguistic features of biographies

Purpose

- To give an account of someone's life

Structure

- Has an opening that introduces the subject and why he/she is known or remembered
- Includes information about significant events, organised chronologically, sometimes accompanied by views of others
- Has concluding or rounding-off remarks; these may sometimes indicate the writer's opinion

Language features

- Refers to named individuals e.g. *Alan Shearer, Peter Shilton*
- Contains dates linked to specific events
- Written in past tense
- Contains time markers e.g. *'He was born in the Gosforth district of the city on 13 August 1970.'*
- Contains a variety of verbs, e.g. action, mental processes
- Can include direct and indirect speech
- May include quotes from other sources, e.g. newspapers
- Written in 3rd person

Annotated model biography text

Text structure and organisation

Language features

Model biography text
Amy Johnson

Introduction

Amy Johnson was the first woman to fly solo from England to Australia.

Early life

Amy was born in 1903 in Hull, where she grew up and went to school. In 1925 she graduated from Sheffield University.

Series of significant events, organised chronologically

Amy then went to London to work as a secretary. She became interested in aviation and, in 1928, she qualified as a pilot. She also became the first British woman to be granted a licence to service planes.

Amy was keen to break the record, held by Jim Mollinson, for a solo flight from England to Australia. On 5 May 1930 she took off for Darwin,

who

what subject is known for

action verbs: past tense

named individuals

specific places

Australia. On 24 May Amy reached Darwin. She had failed to break the record by three days.

Although Amy missed the record, she became very well known for her courage. The British press called her 'Queen of the Air'. The Daily Mail gave her a £10,000 prize, and she was made a CBE.

In 1932 Amy married Jim Mollinson. She made several record breaking flights, both as a solo pilot and with her husband. In 1939, at the outbreak of the Second World War, she joined the Air Transport Auxiliary. On 5 January 1941 Amy was killed when her plane crashed in the Thames Estuary.

Concluding statement

time markers and dates

Unit 1

Alan Shearer: A Biography

Text type: Recount/Biography

Learning Outcomes:

To become familiar with the content, structure and language features typical of biographical writing; to distinguish between biographical and autobiographical writing.

Preparation:

Collect examples of biographical and autobiographical writing. Include in the collection 'fanzines', theatre and football programmes and other publications that contain biographical information.

The written outcome of this unit is individual biographies written by the children. They could all write about the same person, a person of their own choice, a friend or member of their family. You may wish to tie this in with another curriculum area and ask the children to write a biography of a scientist, explorer or inventor.

Show the class the book you are going to study. Explain that you are going to work with enlarged pages from *Alan Shearer: A Biography* to ensure that everyone can see clearly.

Lesson 1

Spotlight on: Immersion

Teaching Objective

- *To distinguish between biography and autobiography (Y6 T1 T11)*

Whole Class Shared Reading

Mask the words *A Biography* on the front cover of the *Alan Shearer: A Biography* big book. Read the title of the book and ask the children what sort of information they would expect to find in the book and who might have written it. List the children's responses.

Look through the book, drawing attention to the headings. Do they help to confirm the children's predictions? Read pages 4 and 5. Ask whether the children think this was written by Alan Shearer. Reveal the rest of the cover title and discuss the terms *biography* and *autobiography*. You may wish to refer to a dictionary to explore the definitions of the

two prefixes. Remind the children of the introduction they read on pages 4 and 5, and the fact that it was written in the third person. Discuss how it would differ if it was written in the first person.

Group Activities

- In pairs, the children can sort through the collection of biographical and autobiographical writing and identify which is which.
- The children can complete PCM 3 (see page 22).

Plenary

Ask several children to report on their findings. Did they have any difficulty in classifying the writing?

The children can give examples with meanings from their completed PCM.

Lesson 2

Spotlight on: Immersion

Teaching Objective

- *To distinguish between biography and autobiography (Y6 T1 T11)*

Whole Class Shared Reading

Ask the children to think about the similarities between biographies and autobiographies. Remind them that, while both are likely to record events, an autobiography is likely to contain incidents, thoughts and feelings known only to the author. A biography includes comments made by others about the subject and is unable to include personal details unless the subject has made them known.

Explain that you are going to look for comments made about Alan Shearer by others. Skim through the pages of the big book to find examples of quotes. Read the quotations and note down some of the words used to describe Shearer. Discuss with the children what they feel they now know about Shearer. Is it fact or opinion?

Group Activities

Individually or in pairs, the children can select words from those noted in the whole class session and define them using General PCM 3 (see page 72).

Plenary

Ask a few children to read out their own definitions. Challenge the rest of the class to decide on their accuracy before reading the dictionary definition.

Lesson ❸

Spotlight on: Discovery

Teaching Objective

- *To distinguish between biography and autobiography (Y6 T1 T11)*

Whole Class Shared Reading

Read the model text on pages 2 and 3 of the big book. Focus on the use of paragraphs. Discuss with the children the main points of each paragraph and write these on the acetate sheet. Discuss the purpose of the text with the children.

Group Activities

Using examples from the collection of biographical and autobiographical writing, ask the children to do a similar analysis of textual organisation.

Plenary

Using the feedback from the children, draw up a framework for a biography. You may wish to use PCM 1 (see page 20) as a model. Use the feedback from the children to reinforce the differences and similarities between recounts and biographies.

Lesson ❹

Spotlight on: Discovery

Teaching Objective

- *To distinguish between biography and autobiography (Y6 T1 T11)*

Whole Class Shared Reading

Before reading, discuss with the children the use of tables and grids to present information, e.g. their purposes, when they are used and which text types are likely to contain them. Look through the pages of the big book and briefly look at and discuss the different tables and grids and the information they give. Discuss how they can contribute to clarity and how complicated or lengthy details can be summarised for the reader to understand at a glance.

Turn to page 9 and read the information in the table. Discuss with the children how the information could be given solely using text. Focus particularly on the map, drawings of the strip and the club badge.

Using the acetate sheet, demonstrate how to highlight key words and phrases on page 8.

Group Activities

The children can complete PCM 4 (see page 23) to summarise and represent detailed information.

Plenary

Ask some children to read out their fact panels. Do other children agree with their analyses? Were there any discrepancies? If so what were they and why were these areas problematic? You may wish to use the feedback to draw up a revision poster on how to extract information.

Lesson ❺

Spotlight on: Familiarisation

Teaching Objectives

- *To distinguish between biography and autobiography (Y6 T1 T11)*
- *To revise word classes, re-expressing sentences, complex sentences, standard English, adapting texts (Y6 T1 S1)*
- *To form complex sentences (Y6 T1 S5)*

Whole Class Shared Reading

Using the model text on pages 2 and 3 of the big book, highlight the language features typical of a biography. Use the annotated version on pages 14 and 15 of this guide to ensure that all the relevant features are covered.

Remind the children of the difference between biography and autobiography and the uses of the 1st and 3rd person. Ensure that children understand the difference between the two voices.

Focus on the connecting words and phrases found in this text and their effect.

Read pages 10 and 11 and ask the children to listen for words and phrases that connect events or ideas. List their suggestions.

Group Activities

- The children can find and list further examples in other biographical texts.
- They can complete PCM 2 (see page 21).
- Some children may extend this to looking for connecting words and phrases in other text types.

Plenary

Ask the children to report on their findings. Add further words and phrases to the chart.

Lesson ⑥

Spotlight on: Familiarisation

Teaching Objective

- *To distinguish between biography and autobiography (Y6 T1 T11)*

Whole Class Shared Reading

Read through all the pages in the *Alan Shearer: A Biography* big book.

Discuss the chronological nature of the text; focus on the use of time markers, e.g. specific dates, *'four years later', 'four days later…'.*

Re-read pages 4 and 5. Discuss the fact that this works as an introduction as it summarises Shearer's life. You may wish to refer back to the framework produced in Lesson 3.

Read the headings and sub-headings on each page. Discuss the author's use of language and the words and phrases associated with football.

Ask the children why many of them sound like newspaper headlines.

Group Activities

The children can break the text on PCM 2 (see page 21) into paragraphs and produce suitable headings for each paragraph. Encourage them to adopt a newspaper headline style.

Plenary

Ask a few children to read out their headings. If necessary write up lengthier examples and, with the children, identify and delete unnecessary words.

Lesson ⑦

Spotlight on: The writing process

Teaching Objective

- *To develop the skills of biographical and autobiographical writing in role, adopting distinctive voices (Y6 T1 T14)*

Whole Class Shared Writing

Explain to the children that they will each be writing a biography over the next four lessons. Introduce and discuss a chosen subject for their biographies. If appropriate, pool existing knowledge about the subject in a class brainstorm. Retain this for future use.

If the children are writing about different subjects, demonstrate how to brainstorm knowledge.

Ask the children what further information they need. Record this in the form of questions.

Discuss with the children where they could find further information on the subject. If appropriate, discuss the possibility of carrying out interviews.

Group Activities

- If the children are all writing about the same subject, they can start to research the subject using the questions produced in the shared writing session as prompts.
- If they are writing about different subjects they can brainstorm existing knowledge and identify further information they require.
- If interviews are appropriate, the children can list questions they would ask.

Plenary

The children can feed back on their progress so far.

Some children can read out their interview questions. Discuss 'open' questions that require more than a yes or no answer.

Lesson ⑧

Spotlight on: The writing process

Teaching Objectives

- *To develop the skills of biographical and autobiographical writing in role, adopting distinctive voices (Y6 T1 T14)*

Whole Class Shared Writing

With the children, organise the class brainstorm into a concept map by grouping information under headings. Retain this for future use.

Ask the children what information, from the concept map, they would include in the introduction to the biography. List this.

If the children are writing about different subjects, discuss how they plan to organise their biographies and demonstrate with one child's brainstorm how to turn it into a concept map.

Group Activities

- If the children are writing about the same subject, they can write a draft introduction from the notes made during shared writing.

- If the children are writing about different subjects, they can turn their brainstorms into concept maps and carry out further research.

Plenary

Discuss with the children any illustrations they might need to add e.g. timelines, family trees, photographs.

Discuss the use of quotes from interviews and other sources.

Lesson 9

Spotlight on: The writing process

Teaching Objective

- *To develop the skills of biographical and autobiographical writing in role, adopting distinctive voices (Y6 T1 T14)*

Whole Class Shared Writing

Discuss with the children how they might include quotes about the subject of their autobiographies, e.g. within the text, boxes around the page.

Focus on the use of speech verbs and alternatives to 'said' e.g. 'recalls', 'remembers', 'comments'. List these and display as a chart.

Ask the children whether they need to include everything that was said in a quote. Remind them of the use of an ellipsis (…) to show that part of a quote has been omitted.

Demonstrate how to turn a quote into reported speech, e.g. *Fred told me how he and Harry used to go apple scrumping.*

Group Activities

The children can continue writing their draft biographies.

Plenary

Ask a few children to read extracts from their biographies. Encourage other children to make constructively critical comments.

If necessary, note any areas that are proving problematical for the children.

Lesson 10

Spotlight on: The writing process

Teaching Objective

- *To develop the skills of biographical and autobiographical writing in role, adopting distinctive voices (Y6 T1 T14)*

Whole Class Shared Writing

With their permission, use an example of a child's writing to demonstrate how to solve any problematical areas noted during Lesson 9.

Alternatively, demonstrate how to edit a section of a draft biography for clarity. Focus on style of writing and language used.

Group Activities

The children can continue to draft and edit their biographies.

Plenary

Discuss final layout and publication, using IT where possible, of children's biographies.

Name

Biography framework

Introduction (who, why or what subject is known for)

Early life

Series of significant events, chronologically organised

Concluding or rounding-off remarks

 PCM ❶

Text type: Biography (*Alan Shearer: A Biography*)
Links with Literacy Lesson: **Year 6, Unit 1, Lesson 3**

Name

Autobiography into biography

Turn this autobiographical account of Alan Shearer's early years into a biographical account.

My name is Alan Shearer. I was born in Newcastle on 13 August 1970. I have always loved football. From the moment I could kick a ball I have played football. As a lad I played every day. It didn't matter if I didn't have a proper ball, I would use a stone or an old can to play with. As a youngster all I ever dreamed about was playing football for Newcastle United and England.

When I was at school, as well as playing in the school teams, I played for two local clubs: Cramlington Juniors and Wallsend Boys Club. When I was fifteen, I was picked to play for the Northumberland Boys Under 19 county team. I was so proud, especially as I was a lot younger and smaller than the rest of the team.

When I was fourteen, I had a trial for Southampton and the club signed me up as an associate schoolboy. In 1986, just before I was sixteen, I signed as a trainee at Southampton and moved south. I stayed with Southampton until 1992 when I was transferred to Blackburn Rovers for a British record transfer fee of £3.3 million.

Text type: Biography (*Alan Shearer: A Biography*)
Links with Literacy Lesson: **Year 6, Unit 1, Lessons 5 and 6**

PCM 2

Name _____

Word web

**Make a word web of words that include
bio, auto and *graph*.**

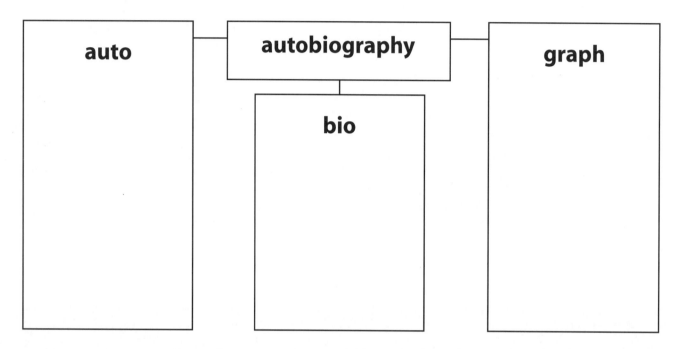

Write a definition of three words from your word web, then check
them in a dictionary.

Check and write the meaning of *auto, bio,* and *graph*.

Use *auto, bio* and *graph* to invent three new words. Write them
down with a definition. Cover your definitions and ask a friend to
work out the meaning of your invented words.

PCM 3

Text type: Biography (*Alan Shearer: A Biography*)
Links with Literacy Lesson: **Year 6, Unit 1, Lesson 1**

Name _____

Information panel

Turn this history of Newtown Football Club into an information panel about the club, like the ones in *Alan Shearer: A Biography*.

Newtown United Football Club

Newtown United Football Club was founded in 1884. The first players all lived in and around the town and most of them were foundry or shipyard workers. In those days, matches and training took place after work, at weekends or on public holidays. The pitch the team played on was Newtown Recreation Ground. Today the club owns its own ground, and, in honour of the club's early days, their home ground is called 'The Rec'. The team strip consists of a navy blue, red and yellow horizontally striped shirt, black shorts and yellow socks. The club badge is a navy blue shield with two stripes, one red, the other yellow, running in parallel diagonally from the top right to the bottom left. Because many of the original Newtown players worked in heavy industry, the team soon became known as 'The Steelmen'. To this day, it remains the team's nickname. Newtown United earned honours locally and today is a nationally recognised team. Six years after the club was founded, United won the prestigious amateur trophy, the North East Cup, a feat they repeated for the following three seasons. This achievement gained them admittance to the Third Division. By 1896, the team's consistent playing and scoring record earned them a place in Division One. In the short space of only three seasons they had moved from local amateur champions to an established First Division club.

Text type: Biography (*Alan Shearer: A Biography*)
Links with Literacy Lesson: **Year 6, Unit 1, Lesson 4**

PCM

© Reed Educational and Professional Publishing Ltd, 1999

Year 6: Unit 2

Report: *Spiders (and how they hunt)*

Introduction

Much of the non-fiction reading and writing that children do in curricular areas other than English can be classified as the report text type. Children will have read and written reports and explored typical structural and linguistic features prior to Year 6.

Spiders (and how they hunt) is a report text that gives information about different spiders and the methods they use to catch their prey. It is organised into sections with main and sub-headings. A variety of illustrations typical of this text type are used, including icons, labelled diagrams, Venn diagrams, a flow chart and tables.

On pages 2 and 3 of the *Spiders (and how they hunt)* big book you will find a model report text. This text has been specially written to contain all the structural and linguistic details typically found in a report. We suggest that you go through this model text with the children, pointing out the typical features of the text type. The sheet of acetate provided with the big books is designed to be placed in front of the model texts so that you can write your own notes and annotations around the text. Further information on using the model text can be found in the notes for Lessons 3 and 4, and on pages 26 and 27 of this guide you will find an annotated version of the same text to help you to draw out its relevant features.

At the end of this unit you may wish to use General PCMs 2, 5, 7 and 8 as part of continuous assessment.

Structural and linguistic features of non-chronological reports

Purpose

- To document, organise and store information

Structure

- Has an opening general statement or definition
- Includes facts about various aspects of the subject grouped into topic areas and organised into paragraphs
- Has a closing general statement

Language features

- Refers to generalised rather than specific participants, e.g. '**Spiders** that hunt their prey'
- Contains some action verbs, e.g. 'Spiders that **catch** their prey'
- Contains some linking verbs, e.g. 'Some people **are** afraid of spiders'
- Usually written in simple present tense
- Contains descriptive language, but factual and precise, e.g. 'Spiders … have huge stabbing fangs'
- Has language for defining, classifying, comparing and contrasting, e.g. '**All** spiders have eight legs', '**Most** spiders have eight eyes', 'There are **significant differences** between the two'
- Contains technical vocabulary, e.g. arachnid, spinnerets, abdomen
- Fairly formal style, usually written in the third person

Annotated model report text

Text structure and organisation

Language features

Model report text
London Zoo

London Zoo is an integral part of the Zoological Society of London, which is a world wide conservation, scientific and educational charity.

London Zoo is one of the most important zoos in the world. It has an extensive breeding and conservation programme. There are over 12,000 animals in the zoo, a considerable number of which (116 animal species and over 1000 bird species) are in danger of extinction in the wild.

However, conservation costs money, so London Zoo has fundraising schemes to help provide some of the finance. These include membership subscriptions, Lifewatch and Animal

Opening statement: simple definition

Facts grouped into topic areas and organised into paragraphs

Formal style: third person

comparative language

linking verbs: present tense

generalised participants

action verbs

Adoption. As well as supporting conservation programmes, the money raised from these schemes helps to pay for veterinary care, breeding programmes and scientific research.

Inside the zoo are numerous animal enclosures and displays. Amongst these are the famous Mappin Terraces. This enclosure was first opened in 1914 as a bear exhibit. Recently it has been redesigned, and today the Mappin Terraces are home to sloth bears, Hanuman langurs and Reeve's muntjac.

London Zoo is situated in Regent's Park, in north west London. It is open every day of the year except Christmas Day and can be reached by tube, bus, waterbus or car.

technical vocabulary

descriptive but factual language

Rounding-off statement

27

Unit 2

Spiders (and how they hunt)

Text type: Report

Learning Outcomes:

To become familiar with the content, structure and language features typical of a non-chronological report, and to learn to write reports.

Preparation:

Make a collection of examples of report texts. These should cover a wide range of subject matters, rather than being confined to reports on animals.

Collect together a variety of leaflets, brochures and pamphlets on tourist attractions. These will tend to contain a mix of text types.

As the written outcome of this unit is a script for a TV documentary on spiders, you will need at least one clip from such a programme.

Show the class the book you are going to study. Explain that you are going to work with enlarged pages from *Spiders (and how they hunt)* to ensure that everyone can see clearly.

Lesson ❶

Spotlight on: Immersion

Teaching Objective

- *To secure understanding of the features of non-chronological reports (Y6 T1 T13)*

Whole Class Shared Reading

Show the children the front cover of the *Spiders (and how they hunt)* big book and read the title.

Ask what kind of information they think will be found in the book.

Discuss which text types might be found in the book. List the children's suggestions.

Turn to the introduction on pages 4 and 5 of the big book, and read it through. Ask the children whether they can identify the text type.

To clarify their understanding of a report text, list the focus of each paragraph e.g. habitat, classification, physical features.

Look at the table on page 4. With the children, identify other places on the spread where some of the facts in the table are given. These could be highlighted using the acetate sheet.

Group Activities

Ask the children to browse through the collection of report texts.

They can choose one book and note down its subject matter, e.g. animal, place, and the features that indicate it is a report. They could use PCM 3 to record their findings (see page 34).

Plenary

Ask a number of children to explain to the rest of the class how the features they have identified indicate that the texts are reports.

Ensure that the children understand that reports can cover a whole range of subjects or topics.

Lesson ❷

Spotlight on: Immersion

Teaching Objective

- *To secure understanding of the features of non-chronological reports (Y6 T1 T13)*

Whole Class Shared Reading

Turn to pages 6 and 7 of the *Spiders (and they hunt)* big book. Focus the children's attention on the heading and sub-headings.

Read the text on page 6. Ask the children whether this is typical of a report. Allow them to justify their comments.

Read the text on page 7. Ask whether this is also typical of a report. Are the children able to comment on the chronological nature of this section which indicates that it is an explanation?

Through discussion, ensure the children are clear on the two text types. Explain that many texts, such as this one, contain a mix of text types as they have a range of purposes.

Recap on the purpose of reports, e.g. to document and organise information on a subject.

Group Activities

Ask the children to look at the collection of report texts and find examples of the inclusion of other text types. They can note down the text type and its purpose.

Plenary

Ask some children to report on their findings.

Explain that reports are not only in written format, but can also be found on TV, video and radio.

Play the children a brief extract from a TV or radio documentary.

Lesson ③

Spotlight on: Discovery

Teaching Objective

- *To secure understanding of the features of non-chronological reports (Y6 T1 T13)*

Whole Class Shared Reading

Turn to the model report text on pages 2 and 3 of the *Spiders (and how they hunt)* big book.

Explain to the children that you are going to look at the way the report is organised.

Read through the model text.

Ask the children to suggest a heading for each paragraph. Write these on the acetate sheet.

Discuss the fact that this is a report on a place, therefore the headings for the paragraphs would not be suitable for a report on animals. Similarly, the headings for a report on animals would not be suitable for a report on places.

With the children, list more general headings that could be used for a report on any subject. See PCM 1 (see page 32) for suggested headings.

Group Activities

The children can look at other examples of reports and list headings for each paragraph. They can use PCM 1 to record their findings.

Ask them to consider the effectiveness of the structure of the reports.

Plenary

Ask the children to feed back the headings they have listed.

Discuss the fact that the order in which facts are grouped is flexible, but that facts on one aspect of a subject are usually grouped into one paragraph.

Are the children able to be critical of the reports they looked at, identifying strengths and weaknesses?

Ask the children what they know about the language features that are typical of a report. List their responses and keep this for the following lesson.

Lesson ④

Spotlight on: Discovery

Teaching Objectives

- *To secure understanding of the features of non-chronological reports (Y6 T1 T13)*
- *To form complex sentences (Y6 T1 S5)*

Whole Class Shared Reading

Return to the model text on pages 2 and 3 of the big book.

Explain that you are going to highlight language features that are typical of reports.

Return to the list produced during the Plenary session of Lesson 3. Work through this list and, using the acetate sheet, identify examples of the features the children suggested.

Refer to the annotated version of the model text on pages 26 and 27 of this guide and highlight any features that have not already been identified.

Group Activities

Give the children a range of leaflets, pamphlets and brochures.

Working in pairs, they can highlight the elements within them that are typical of reports. They can use PCM 3 to record their findings (see page 34).

The children can also list other text types they find within the collection, e.g. instructions for finding a place, persuasive devices to encourage visitors, recount of the history of the attraction.

Plenary

A small number of children can feed back on their findings to the rest of the class.

Lesson ⑤

Spotlight on: Familiarisation

Teaching Objectives

- *To secure understanding of the features of non-chronological reports (Y6 T1 T13)*
- *To form complex sentences (Y6 T1 S5)*

Whole Class Shared Reading

Read through the text on pages 8 and 9 of the big book.

Turn to pages 10 and 11 and read through the text on these pages.

Ask the children what differences they notice in the use of headings and sub-headings between these two double page spreads.

Turn to pages 12 and 13. Allow the children to look at the Venn diagram for a few minutes, and then ask them to explain the information given.

Discuss other ways that this information could be presented.

Focus on page 7 and, using the acetate sheet, highlight the complex sentence in section 1 starting *'When an insect lands on the tube…'*.

With the children, identify the connectives *however* and *so*. Do they have the same meaning?

Discuss how different connectives have different meanings and can change the overall meaning of a sentence.

Start to build up a collection of wall charts of connectives, categorised by meaning. Encourage the children to add to them from their reading.

Group Activities

The children can complete PCM 2 and PCM 4.

Plenary

Ask a small number of children to read out their PCM.

Discuss with the class which connectives were the most appropriate. Draw out of the discussion the differences in the various connectives, e.g. time, cause and effect, comparison, additional information.

What text types do the children think they have created? How did they reach their conclusions?

Further information on connectives is available in the NLS *Framework for teaching* glossary.

Lesson 6

Spotlight on: Familiarisation

Teaching Objectives

- *To secure understanding of the features of non-chronological reports (Y6 T1 T13)*
- *To develop a journalistic style (Y6 T1 T15)*

Whole Class Shared Reading

Explain to the children that you are going to watch a brief clip from a TV documentary. Give them some background details, i.e. content and subject matter, to put the clip into a context.

Show the clip with the sound turned off.

Ask what kind of commentary or voiceover they would expect to hear.

Tell the children that you are going to replay the clip with the sound turned on. Ask them to listen carefully to the information they are given.

You may then wish to display headings that the children could use to organise their notes as they watch the clip for a third time.

Group Activities

In pairs, the children can discuss and compare information they noted.

Plenary

As a class, discuss the purpose of voiceovers on documentaries.

Discuss the differences between spoken and written reports, e.g. written reports contain complex sentences, spoken reports are less formal and contain simpler sentences.

Lesson 7

Spotlight on: The writing process

Teaching Objectives

- *To develop a journalistic style (Y6 T1 T15)*
- *To use the styles and conventions of journalism to report on real or imagined events (Y6 T1 T16)*
- *To write non-chronological reports linked to other subjects (Y6 T1 T17)*
- *To use IT to bring writing to publication standard (Y6 T1 T18)*

Whole Class Shared Writing

Explain to the children that, over the next four lessons, they will be working towards writing a voiceover, in the style of a report, for a documentary.

Discuss the unknown audience that TV writers must consider and how this will affect the tone and style of the report.

You could either identify a particular audience or have an unknown audience for this writing.

You could ask each group of children to focus on writing a voiceover based on one double page spread, or on the complete big book. Alternatively, you may wish to link this writing activity with another curriculum area, or provide a clip from a documentary without the voiceover.

Look at each double page spread in the big book, focusing on and listing the visual elements, e.g. on pages 4 and 5: photo of spider, table of features, diagram of body parts.

Discuss and list with the children the main points that could be made in the voiceover for each page.

Group Activities

In groups, the children can plan their voiceovers in more detail, listing the key facts they need to include.

Plenary

Each group can feed back on their plans.

Encourage the other children to make comments on the relevance of the points they have included and how they might structure their writing.

Lesson 8

Spotlight on: The writing process

Teaching Objectives

- *To develop a journalistic style (Y6 T1 T15)*
- *To use the styles and conventions of journalism to report on real or imagined events (Y6 T1 T16)*
- *To write non-chronological reports linked to other subjects (Y6 T1 T17)*
- *To use IT to bring writing to publication standard (Y6 T1 T18)*

Whole Class Shared Writing

Discuss with the children how they can turn their plans into a fuller script.

Use examples from the groups' plans to model the process.

Discuss the difference between reading from a written report and reading from a report that is intended to be spoken. You may need to read from a text and play an extract from the documentary clip to emphasise this.

Draw attention to the use of expression in the voiceover.

Group Activities

The children can carry out this drafting process for their own voiceovers.

Plenary

Ask some groups to read extracts from their draft scripts. Encourage the other children to comment on the style and tone of the writing.

Note down positive comments and effective examples for use in the following lesson.

Comment on expression and intonation when reading aloud.

Lesson 9

Spotlight on: The writing process

Teaching Objectives

- *To develop a journalistic style (Y6 T1 T15)*
- *To use the styles and conventions of journalism to report on real or imagined events (Y6 T1 T16)*
- *To write non-chronological reports linked to other subjects (Y6 T1 T17)*
- *To use IT to bring writing to publication standard (Y6 T1 T18)*

Whole Class Shared Writing

Refer back to the list made during the Plenary session of the previous lesson. Draw attention to phrases and techniques that were successful.

Focus on the use of technical vocabulary, and ask the children to consider whether this needs to be defined in the voiceover, bearing in mind the fact that the audience will not have access to a glossary.

Demonstrate how to refine a draft by referring to specific examples from the groups' scripts.

Group Activities

The children can refine their drafts. They will need to consider the overall organisation, the use of typical report language features and technical vocabulary.

Plenary

The groups can run through their voiceovers.

Encourage the other children to comment on the effectiveness of the presentation.

Lesson 10

Spotlight on: The writing process

Teaching Objectives

- *To develop a journalistic style (Y6 T1 T15)*
- *To use the styles and conventions of journalism to report on real or imagined events (Y6 T1 T16)*
- *To write non-chronological reports linked to other subjects (Y6 T1 T17)*
- *To use IT to bring writing to publication standard (Y6 T1 T18)*

Whole Class Shared Writing

This lesson can be used to allow children to practise and present their documentary voiceovers.

You may wish to develop their scripts further by asking them to consider what accompanying instructions would be needed if this was to be turned into a brief for a TV documentary, e.g. camera shots, music, sound effects, credits.

Group Activities

The children can add further details to their scripts, considering how they could add to the atmosphere of the documentary.

Plenary

Ask the groups to explain their choice of details and how they would envisage the final documentary.

Name

Report framework

Introduction

Facts

Facts

Facts

Text type: Report (*Spiders (and how they hunt)*)
Links with Literacy Lesson: **Year 6, Unit 2, Lesson 3**

Complex sentences

Use the connectives to combine these phrases into continuous text. Try to make them as interesting and varied as possible. Think about whether any words should be removed or changed and whether any of the sentences or words should be put into a different order.

Connectives:
in addition, also, as well as
the moment, finally, straightaway, when, next, secondly, afterwards, first, then, eventually
as a consequence, in order to, consequently, as a result, because, nevertheless
differ from, however, whereas, on the other hand, unlike

Phrases:

* the water spider waits for prey to approach
  it senses an insect crawl near
  the spider attacks and bites its prey, injecting it with poison
  the spider returns to is nest to feed

* the bolas spider uses a bolas to catch prey
  it spins the bolas
  it hangs it down like a fishing line
  an insect flies near
  the spider swings the bolas at it
  the insect is caught on the sticky end of the bolas
  the spider pulls the thread and bites the insect

* wolf spiders have long legs
  wolf spiders have large eyes
  they can run fast both on land and across water
  their large eyes allow all round vision

* net throwing spiders differ from other spiders
  other spiders spin webs and sit in them
  net throwing spiders spin webs which they hold in their front legs
  net throwing spiders are nocturnal
  most other spiders

When you have finished, compare your sentences with a partner and discuss which text type you have created.

Text type: Report (*Spiders (and how they hunt)*)
Links with Literacy Lesson: **Year 6, Unit 2, Lesson 5**

PCM 2

© Reed Educational and Professional Publishing Ltd, 1999

Name _____

Report chart

Title	Subject matter	Features that indicate it is a report	Other text types included

PCM ❸

Text type: Report (*Spiders (and how they hunt)*)
Links with Literacy Lesson: **Year 6, Unit 2, Lessons 1 and 4**

Name

Transport Venn diagram

This Venn diagram will show features of different forms of transport. Fill in the blank diagram below with the different features and forms of transport. One example has been done for you.

Features

TRAVELS IN THE AIR

TRAVELS ON LAND

TRAVELS BY SEA

HAS AN ENGINE

Forms of transport

Plane   Bus

Car   Hang-glider

Yacht   Ship

Bicycle   Train

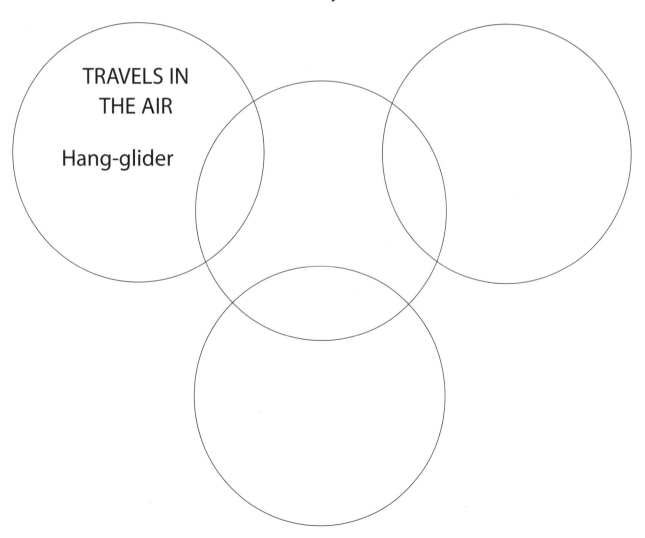

TRAVELS IN
THE AIR

Hang-glider

Text type: Report (*Spiders (and how they hunt)*)
Links with Literacy Lesson: **Year 6, Unit 2, Lesson 5**

PCM **4**

Year 6: Unit 3

Discussion: *Big Issues*

Introduction

Prior to Year 6, children will have read and written both persuasive and discussion/argument texts. They will also have examined typical structural and linguistic features. Children are also aware of these text types through oral work.

Big Issues focuses on four issues, presenting both biased and balanced viewpoints as, for example, letters and commentaries.

On pages 2 and 3 of the *Big Issues* big book you will find a model discussion text. This text has been specially written to contain all the structural and linguistic details typically found in a discussion text. We suggest that you go through this model text with the children, pointing out the typical features of the text type. The sheet of acetate provided with the big books is designed to be placed in front of the model texts so that you can write your own notes and annotations around the text. Further information on using the model text can be found in the notes for Lessons 3 and 4, and on pages 38 and 39 of this guide you will find an annotated version of the same text to help you to draw out its relevant features.

At the end of this unit you may wish to use General PCMs 2, 5, 7 and 8 as part of continuous assessment.

Structural and linguistic features of discussion texts

Purpose

- To take a position on an issue and justify it

Structure

- Opens with a statement of the issue being addressed
- Goes on to state the author's position on the issue
- Contains argument(s) with supporting evidence, reasons and statistics
- Ends with a summary

Language features

- Includes a variety of verbs – action, speech
- Uses sequential phrases and cohesive ties, e.g. *'The opposite view is'*, *'In addition'*, *'On the other hand'*
- Mainly written in simple present tense, but may change according to presentation of points
- Uses language associated with reasoning, e.g. *means that, if, therefore*
- Uses emotive language, e.g. *'Thousands of animals suffer each day.'*
- Uses technical vocabulary, e.g. *transplants, vivisection, vaccines*

Annotated model discussion text

Text structure and organisation

Language features

Model discursive text

The countryside and leisure

Statement of issue

There (are) arguments both for and against developing leisure facilities in the countryside.

Present tense

Arguments for and elaboration

(One view) (is) that the countryside provides, and always should provide, an area of recreation for the increasing numbers of people who live in towns and cities. People today have more leisure time and the countryside is simply changing to meet their demands. Wilderness areas are still there for people to find if they wish, but there is now a wider variety of leisure activities available in the countryside as a whole. (This is to be welcomed,) as it gives visitors more

Cohesive ties and sequential phrases

Some passives

Arguments against and elaboration

Summary

choice as to where to go and how to spend their time.

(Another view) is that as the countryside changes, (it changes forever.) Quiet places are far less easy to find. Many companies, keen to develop in rural areas, have no interest in anyone's (desire to be alone) when this is set against the chance to make money. An increasing number of visitors to the countryside causes severe (environmental damage) and (pollution.) Too much development, too many unpleasant buildings and roads clogged with traffic (may well be) the (bleak) prospect for our countryside.

(It would seem that) opinion is divided on this issue. What is important is to recognise the needs of all people while considering the effect on the countryside.

Cohesive ties and sequential phrases

Emotive language

Technical vocabulary

Conditionals

Language associated with reasoning

Unit 3

Big Issues

Text type: Discussion

Learning Outcomes:

To become familiar with the content, structure and language features typical of a discussion text, and to learn to write discussion texts.

Preparation:

Make a collection of discussion texts.

Show the class the book you are going to study. Explain that you are going to work with enlarged pages from *Big Issues* to ensure that everyone can see clearly.

Lesson 1

Spotlight on: Immersion

Teaching Objective

- *To recognise how arguments are constructed to be effective (Y6 T2 T15)*

Whole Class Shared Reading

Discuss the title of the book. Ask the children what they think it means.

Explore the use of the word *big*. What makes an issue big? Is it big for everybody?

Does the title indicate agreement over issues or author bias?

Explain that the small version of *Big Issues* is about several issues, but the extracts in the big book focus on a single issue.

Read the introduction on page 4 of the big book. Ask the children to notice the key points the author makes about presenting a case and persuading others to accept a personal viewpoint.

Re-read the five numbered points. With the children, identify the main element in each. Use the acetate sheet to highlight or underline them.

Demonstrate how to extract the underlined information to produce a chart, giving guidance on putting forward a point of view.

Group Activities

The children can work individually or in pairs to produce a poster identifying the major points to bear in mind when writing a discussion text.

Plenary

Look at several of the children's posters.

You may wish to take information from a number of these to complete a class poster or display a selection produced by the children.

Lesson 2

Spotlight on: Immersion

Teaching Objective

- *To identify the features of balanced written arguments (Y6 T2 T16)*

Whole Class Shared Reading

Read through pages 5 to 10 of the *Big Issues* big book. With the children, list the eight headings and sub-headings on these pages.

Discuss the section heading – *Vivisection* – and talk about what the word means.

Discuss each heading and its related sub-headings. What would the children expect to read about under each?

Note suggestions next to the relevant heading.

Read through the text on page 5. Ask the children to identify the two points of view taken.

Group Activities

Split the class in half. Ask one half to prepare an argument in support of vivisection and the other to prepare an argument against it.

Plenary

As a class, orally debate the issue of vivisection.

Lesson 3

Spotlight on: Discovery

Teaching Objectives

- *To recognise how arguments are constructed to be effective (Y6 T2 T15)*
- *To identify the features of balanced written arguments (Y6 T2 T16)*

Whole Class Shared Reading

Mask all but the title of the model discussion text on pages 2 and 3 of the *Big Issues* big book.

Read the title and ask the children to think about the what the author's intention might be, e.g. to present one side of an issue or to present a balanced view.

Ask whether it is possible to work out the author's intention from the title.

Reveal and read the text. Help the children to clarify their understanding of the title in relation to the text. Do they now think the title suggests that the author is neutral, or that he or she is biased?

Work through each paragraph and, with the children, identify the purpose of each. (See annotated version of the model text on pages 38 and 39 of this guide.)

Record the framework on a large sheet of paper to use as the basis for a working display.

Group Activities

The children can list, in note form, the main points of the model text under the headings *Arguments for* and *Arguments against*.

They may like to add further arguments for and against developing leisure facilities in the countryside of their own.

Plenary

Review the children's analysis of the arguments and any additions they may have made.

Help them to make connections with previous work on sub-headings done in Lesson 2.

Remind the children how the structure of a discussion text differs from that of a persuasive text, i.e. it includes both sides of an argument.

Lesson

Spotlight on: Discovery

Teaching Objectives

- *To recognise how arguments are constructed to be effective (Y6 T2 T15)*
- *To build a bank of useful terms and phrases for argument (Y6 T2 W8)*

Whole Class Shared Reading

Return to the model text on pages 2 and 3 of the big book.

With the children, identify the language features typical of an argument. Refer to the annotated version of the model text on pages 38 and 39 of this guide if you wish.

Highlight the features using the acetate sheet, then make a permanent record.

Encourage the children to identify further examples within the model text, e.g. other examples of emotive language.

Remind the children that these are also the features of a persuasive text.

Group Activities

Using PCM 2, (see page 45) or examples of persuasive or discussion texts from your collection, the children can identify and highlight typical language features.

Plenary

Ask the children to feed back some of their examples to the rest of the class.

Start to create wall charts of examples of the various features. Display these and encourage children to add to them from their reading.

Lesson 5

Spotlight on: Familiarisation

Teaching Objective

- *To recognise how arguments are constructed to be effective (Y6 T2 T15)*

Whole Class Shared Reading

On the board or a large sheet of paper, draw a chart like that on PCM 3 (see page 46). Write *Supporting material* at the top of the first column, but leave the other two columns blank for now.

With the children, look through the big book pages and draw attention to the ways the author enhances and supports the arguments with illustrations, statistics, quotes, references, etc.

List all these different types of supporting material in the first column of the chart.

Write *What it shows* and *Intended effect* at the top of the other two columns on the chart.

Return to the first entry in the *Supporting material* column. Discuss what is shown and what they think its intended effect is, e.g. the quotes from *Animal Kind* on page 9 add authority.

Record suggestions under the relevant headings on the chart.

Work through the rest of the entries in the *Supporting material* column. Complete the *What it shows* column for each entry.

Encourage the children to be as specific as possible about what is shown.

Group Activities

- The children can complete the *Intended effect* column on PCM 3 (see page 46).
- They can also complete PCM 4.

Plenary

Ask one or two children to present their decisions about the intended effects of the supporting material.

Remind the children about why authors choose to use these devices.

Turn to the bibliography on page 13 of the big book and discuss why authors use sources of information. Is the inclusion of the bibliography also a persuasive device? (It helps to add authority to the book.)

You may wish to add suggestions for additional supporting material to be added to the framework developed in Lesson 3.

Lesson 6

Spotlight on: Familiarisation

Teaching Objectives

- *To understand features of formal official language (Y6 T2 S2)*
- *To recognise how arguments are constructed to be effective (Y6 T2 T15)*

Whole Class Shared Reading

Read through pages 11 and 12 of the big book.

Discuss what '*a wider audience*' means.

Re-read each paragraph and identify the different suggestions for reaching a wider audience. List these.

Draw attention to how this text differs from the rest of the book. Are the children able to recognise the instructional tone? Remind them of the term 'imperative'.

Read through the suggested ways of reaching a wider audience.

Ask the children to suggest what the word *canvass* means. Note their suggestions. Repeat this with one or two other words from these pages.

Group Activities

The children can complete General PCM 3 (see page 72), using words from the list of ways of reaching a wider audience. They should use dictionaries to check their ideas.

Plenary

Review the children's work on the PCM.

Compare the suggested strategies with those used in oral debates, i.e. wider audience versus immediate audience.

Lesson 7

Spotlight on: The writing process

Teaching Objective

- *To construct effective arguments (Y6 T2 T18)*

Whole Class Shared Writing

Identify an issue that the class can present a balanced argument about. You may wish to take another issue from *Big Issues*, one of particular relevance locally, or one related to another subject area.

Using the framework produced in Lesson 3, plan one side of the argument by listing supporting points under the *Arguments for* heading. Demonstrate how to record these points in note form rather than as complete sentences.

Discuss the elements that would be included in the opening statement, and note these under the heading *Statement of issue*.

Group Activities

Using the writing frame on PCM 1 (see page 44) where necessary, the children can plan the opposite point of view.

They can record their arguments in note form under the *Arguments against* heading.

Plenary

Ask the children to read their notes. Discuss the value of the points they have made and record the most effective on the class framework.

Lesson 8

Spotlight on: The writing process

Teaching Objectives

- *To construct effective arguments (Y6 T2 T18)*
- *To use reading to investigate conditionals (Y6 T2 S5)*

Whole Class Shared Writing

Return to the notes made on the framework in the whole class session of Lesson 7.

Demonstrate how to write up the notes into sentences. Encourage the children to refer to the lists of language features developed in Lesson 4 and to suggest ways of using them effectively.

Group Activities

The children can repeat this process with their own plans produced in Lesson 7.

Plenary

Ask the children for suggestions for writing a summary paragraph to the class argument text.
 List their suggestions.

Lesson 9

Spotlight on: The writing process

Teaching Objectives

- *To construct effective arguments (Y6 T2 T18)*
- *To use reading to investigate conditionals (Y6 T2 S5)*

Whole Class Shared Writing

Demonstrate writing up the notes for the summary paragraph into full sentences. Refer to the lists of language features developed in Lesson 4.

Group Activities

In pairs, the children can discuss improvements that could be made to the whole class argument. They should consider whether the points made are developed effectively, whether they are persuasively worded and whether the text offers a balanced viewpoint.

Plenary

As a class, edit the draft argument using improvements identified by the children during the Group Activities session.
 Ask whether the children think you should include any supporting material, e.g. tables, statistics, quotes.

Lesson 10

Spotlight on: The writing process

Teaching Objectives

- *To construct effective arguments (Y6 T2 T18)*
- *To use reading to investigate conditionals (Y6 T2 S5)*

Whole Class Shared Writing

Re-read pages 11 and 12 to refresh the children's memories about how to strengthen an argument.
 As a class, discuss the overall effectiveness of the class argument text.
 Identify whether any of the arguments are particularly weak, anticipate possible objections and, if necessary, strengthen or remove the arguments.

Group Activities

In pairs or groups, the children can discuss and note what they found particularly easy and difficult about writing arguments.

Plenary

Ask some of the children to read their notes from the Group Activities session.
 Review the purpose of discussion texts and when they would be written and read.

Name

Discussion framework

Statement of issue

Arguments for and elaboration

Arguments against and elaboration

Summary

Text type: Discussion (*Big Issues*)
Links with Literacy Lesson: **Year 6, Unit 3, Lesson 7**

Language features of discussion texts

Highlight the typical language features of a discussion text.

Is it right to experiment on animals?

Every year over 3.5 million animals are used for research purposes in British laboratories. A large number of these experiments are for the purposes of medical research and many animals die in the search for new drugs to cure diseases.

Experimentation on living animals is called vivisection. Rats and mice are most commonly used in vivisection, although dogs, cats, monkeys, birds, frogs, rabbits and armadillos may also be used at times. Many experiments involve animals being used in operations or infected with dangerous diseases.

While most people now agree that testing cosmetics on animals is undesirable, opinion is still split as to whether animals should be used in medical research.

Many people would argue that animals' lives should be sacrificed so that human beings may be saved. They believe that humans are special and should take priority over other animals. Supporters of vivisection claim that it has resulted in enormous advances in preventative and curative health care for humans.

The opposite view is that all the Earth's creatures have equal rights and humans have no moral right to use animals for medical experiments solely for the benefit of humans. Scientists have been experimenting on animals for decades, but still have not found cures for the major killers – cancer, heart disease and AIDS.

Can vivisection be justified?

Text type: Discussion (*Big Issues*)
Links with Literacy Lesson: **Year 6, Unit 3, Lesson 4**

PCM

Name

Supporting material

Intended effect	
What it shows	
Supporting material	

Text type: Discussion (*Big Issues*)
Links with Literacy Lesson: **Year 6, Unit 3, Lesson 5**

Name

Reconstructing discussion texts

Keeping caged birds

Many people keep caged birds as pets. They can provide company and entertainment. For many people, a pet bird relieves loneliness as it is an ever-present companion and listener. But we need to reconsider people's desire to keep birds in cages.

Birds are part of the ecological balance of the world. It is their movement that ensures the pollination of plants and the control of pests that would otherwise destroy plants and crops. Without the activity of birds, insect pests will increase and crops will fail.

If birds are kept in cages, they are unable to fly freely and breed. This is likely to lead to problems. Lack of freedom to breed will eventually lead to some species becoming extinct. At a time when the world is losing many species each year, we should be doing all we can to save them.

If birds are kept in cages, their freedom is limited and their flying ability decreases. Eventually some birds could lose the ability to fly further than the width of their cages.

Keeping birds in cages is unnatural. Birds flying freely allow us to admire their grace and beauty and allow them to play their part in the balance of nature.

Text type: Discussion (*Big Issues*)
Links with Literacy Lesson: **Year 6, Unit 3, Lesson 5**

PCM **4**

© Reed Educational and Professional Publishing Ltd, 1999

Year 6: Unit 4

Explanation: *Quakes, Floods and Other Disasters*

Introduction

Some children find that explanations can be difficult both to identify and to write. Structurally they are similar to reports; indeed explanations are often found within reports. The key is to identify the purpose of explanations, i.e. they explain a process, and specific language features, i.e. the use of cause and effect connectives. Prior to Year 6, children will have focused on the use of visuals that explain a process, e.g. flow charts and diagrams, written and read letters that explain, and investigated typical structural and linguistic features.

Quakes, Floods and Other Disasters explains what causes some natural disasters, and the effects they have on people and the environment.

On pages 2 and 3 of the *Quakes, Floods and Other Disasters* big book you will find a model explanation text. This text has been specially written to contain all the structural and linguistic details typically found in an explanation. We suggest that you go through this model text with the children, pointing out the typical features of the text type. The sheet of acetate provided with the big books is designed to be placed in front of the model texts so that you can write your own notes and annotations around the text. Further information on using the model text can be found in the notes for Lesson 1, and on pages 50 and 51 of this guide you will find an annotated version of the same text to help you to draw out its relevant features.

As well as revising and extending children's knowledge of explanations, the activities for this book also provide opportunities to consolidate and apply knowledge of other text types.

At the end of this unit you may wish to use General PCMs 2, 5, 7 and 8 as part of continuous assessment.

Structural and linguistic features of explanation texts

Purpose

- To give an account of how or why something works or happens

Structure

- Has an opening statement about the process
- Consists of a sequenced explanation, often chronological

Language features

- Contains mainly action verbs, e.g. *'Air **moves** in from an area of high pressure'*
- Usually uses timeless present tense
- Sometimes uses passive voice, e.g. *'A tsunami can be caused by an earthquake.'*
- The passage of time is often implied, particularly when explaining a process, e.g. *The sea bed heaves, and so does the water above it. This starts a long, low wave that ripples out at great speed towards the coast. The wave can travel at several hundred kilometres per hour. As the tsunami approaches the shore, it moves over shallower water and begins to build up.'*
- Includes cause and effect relationships, e.g. *'When the air is cold, the molecules are very close together. When the air is warm, the molecules spread out.'*
- Usually written in the 3rd person
- Includes generalised, non-human participants, e.g. *the wind, volcanoes, earthquakes*

Annotated model explanation text

Model explanation text
How a training shoe works

The main purpose of a sports training shoe is to protect the wearer's feet and legs. A runner's foot hits the ground with a great deal of force, so there is a danger that muscles and joints may be damaged.

The various parts of a trainer provide different kinds of support. Inside the back of the shoe is a hard section called a heel counter. This is designed in order to stop sideways movements of the foot, which could cause damage to the heel or knee.

The sole supports and cushions the foot. As it needs to absorb the shock of impact on the foot and leg muscles, the first layer is thick and

Opening statement

Sequenced explanation

Action verbs: present tense

Cause and effect connectives

soft. The second layer is made of a hard material, such as carbon rubber, (so that) it will resist wear. To make it flexible and provide grip, the sole is grooved. On some trainers, the sole extends around the toe and heel to provide extra grip.

The side panels of many trainers are made of lightweight nylon which is finely meshed. (As a consequence) of this, heat and moisture are allowed to escape and air to circulate. This helps to keep the feet dry and free from blisters.

A sports trainer (is carefully designed) and made. Each part (is constructed) so that the wearer can perform well without damaging limbs, muscles or joints.

Unit 4

Quakes, Floods and Other Disasters

Text type: Explanation

Learning Outcomes:

To become familiar with the content, structure and language features of explanation texts, and to learn to write explanation texts.

Preparation:

The outcome of this unit is a quiz book containing explanations. You will need to identify work in another subject area that lends itself to this text type, e.g. science, geography, history. Collect examples of books that contain a variety of quizzes.

Show the class the book you are going to study. Explain that you are going to work with enlarged pages from *Quakes, Floods and Other Disasters* to ensure that everyone can see clearly.

Lesson ①

Spotlight on: Immersion

Teaching Objectives

- *To secure understanding of the features of explanatory texts from Year 5 Term 2 (Y6 T3 T15)*
- *To review a range of non-fiction text types and their characteristics, discussing when a writer might choose to write in a given style and form (Y6 T3 T19)*
- *To revise the language and grammatical features of the different types of text (Y6 T3 S1)*

Whole Class Shared Reading

Show the children the front cover of the *Quakes, Floods and Other Disasters* big book. Ask what text type or types they think might be found in the book, based on the title and the photograph on the cover.

As they suggest a text type, ask the children to quickly summarise the structure and language features associated with it.

Turn to the model text on pages 2 and 3 of the big book. Ask the children to identify the text type, and revise the structure and language features of explanations. If necessary, use PCM 1 (see page 56) as the basis for the structure.

Explain to the children that you want to see whether the whole book is an explanation, or whether it includes other text types. Turn to pages 4 and 5 of the big book. Look at the way the information is organised on the page and read the sub-headings. Which text types can be ruled out?

Read the first section, *Measuring the wind*. Discuss the text type with the children. Are they able to identify that this is a report?

Read the second and third sections, *What makes the wind blow?* and *Why does a tornado cause such damage?* Ask whether these too are reports. Are the children able to identify these as explanations?

Discuss the differences between the three sub-headings on the page.

Focus on the visual elements. Ask which supports the report (the table of the Beaufort Scale) and which supports the explanations (the hurricane diagram).

Group Activities

The children can complete PCM 2 (see page 57).

Plenary

Discuss with the children the fact that many books contain a mix of text types depending upon their purpose.

Lesson ②

Spotlight on: Immersion

Teaching Objectives

- *To identify the key features of impersonal formal language, e.g. the present tense, the passive voice, and discuss when and why they are used (Y6 T3 T16)*
- *To secure the skills of skimming, scanning and efficient reading so that research is fast and effective (Y6 T3 T18)*

Whole Class Shared Reading

Turn to pages 8 and 9 of the big book. Ask the children to skim the pages, reading the headings quickly. Close the book. What information would they expect to find on these pages? List the children's responses.

Return to pages 8 and 9. Read each paragraph. Are the children's predictions confirmed?

If necessary, revise the construction of a passive sentence, giving a couple of examples.

Focus on the sentence beginning *'About 6000 holiday caravans…'*. Ask the children to transform the sentence into the active voice. Write up their suggestions. Discuss how the impact is reduced. Repeat this activity with the final sentence, beginning *'The best answer…'*. Discuss the clumsiness of the result.

Group Activities

- The children can look at non-fiction texts related to other subjects, identifying passive sentences, transforming them into the active voice and discussing the result.
- The children can complete PCM 3 (see page 58).

Plenary

With the children, summarise the linguistic features typical of an explanation (see annotated model explanation text on pages 50 and 51 of this guide). You may wish to list these and display them for future reference.

Lesson ❸

Spotlight on: Familiarisation

Teaching Objectives

- *To appraise a text quickly and effectively; to retrieve information from it; to find information quickly and evaluate its value (Y6 T3 T17)*
- *To secure the skills of skimming, scanning and efficient reading so that research is fast and effective (Y6 T3 T18)*

Whole Class Shared Reading

Turn to page 4 of the big book. With the children, read through the *Facts* box.

Turn to pages 6 and 7 of the big book.

Explain that, as a class, you are going to produce a fact box about tsunamis, and that the children should listen for facts. Read through pages 6 and 7.

Ask which facts the children think should be included in the box. Using the acetate sheet, highlight key words and phrases.

Ask the children whether they think any information from the diagram could be included in the facts box.

Group Activities

In small groups, the children can produce fact boxes based on the key words and phrases highlighted. They should give the box a title.

Ask the children to write their fact boxes as a poster. Alternatively, they could write on an acetate sheet for use on an OHP in the plenary session.

Plenary

The children can present their fact boxes to the rest of the class, discussing their choice of wording.

Lesson ❹

Spotlight on: Familiarisation

Teaching Objectives

- *To secure understanding of the features of explanatory texts from Year 5 Term 2 (Y6 T3 T15)*
- *To appraise a text quickly and effectively; to retrieve information from it; to find information quickly and evaluate its value (Y6 T3 T17)*
- *To secure the skills of skimming, scanning and efficient reading so that research is fast and effective (Y6 T3 T18)*

Whole Class Shared Reading

Remind the children that typical features of an explanation are flow charts and diagrams.

Using pages 6 and 7 of the big book, explain that you are going to read through the explanation of what causes a tsunami, and then represent it as a flow chart.

Use the acetate sheet to highlight key information.

Discuss the features of a flow chart with the children. e.g. they are sequential, they have brief labels explaining cause and effect.

Group Activities

The children can reinterpret the highlighted information as a flow chart. It would be useful for the charts to be produced as posters or as an OHT.

Plenary

Children can present and explain their flow charts. Discuss features they have included, e.g. how they indicated the start of the sequence, the number of steps, the clarity of the labelling.

Lesson ❺

Spotlight on: Familiarisation

Teaching Objectives

- *To review a range of non-fiction text types and their characteristics, discussing when a writer might choose to write in a given style and form (Y6 T3 T19)*
- *To select the appropriate style and form to suit a specific purpose and audience, drawing on knowledge of different non-fiction text types (Y6 T3 T22)*
- *To revise the language conventions and grammatical features of the different types of text (Y6 T3 S1)*

Whole Class Shared Reading

Read pages 10 and 11 of the big book. Discuss the children's understanding of global warming.

Focus on the final sentence, 'If all this happens…'. Ask the children why they think the author included this sentence and what his view on global warming might be.

Re-read the second and third sections on these pages, *What causes global warming?* and *What effects will global warming have in the future?* Ask the children to identify the text type (explanation). Discuss how these sections could be re-presented as a piece of persuasive writing.

Discuss what the purpose of this piece of persuasive writing would be, e.g. to persuade people to reduce the emission of greenhouse gases.

Discuss and note the structure and language features of persuasive texts.

Ask the children how the issue under discussion could be introduced.

Group Activities

The children can plan and draft a piece of persuasive writing using the information from these two sections. Some children may need the support of PCM 4 (see page 59).

Plenary

Discuss with the children the most effective form for presenting their persuasive writing, e.g. poster, letter, leaflet. Draw out the effect the audience would have on choice of form.

Lesson 6

Spotlight on: Familiarisation

Teaching Objectives

- *To review a range of non-fiction text types and their characteristics, discussing when a writer might choose to write in a given style and form (Y6 T3 T19)*
- *To secure control of impersonal writing, particularly the sustained use of the present tense and the passive voice (Y6 T3 T20)*
- *To revise the language conventions and grammatical features of the different types of text (Y6 T3 S1)*

Whole Class Shared Reading

Revisit pages 10 and 11 of the big book. Demonstrate to the children how it is possible to indicate an alternative point of view by changing the final sentence. Using the acetate sheet, edit the final sentence to read 'This happens because people need to survive.'

Discuss how the sections *What causes global warming?* and *What effects will global warming have in the future?* could be re-presented as a balanced argument.

Discuss and note the structure and language features of discursive texts and how they differ from persuasive writing.

As a class, write the introduction for a balanced argument about global warming.

Group Activities

The children can plan and draft a balanced argument about global warming.

Plenary

Discuss with the children any difficulties they had in trying to maintain an objective view and trying to present the issue as a balanced argument. Focus on the use of the impersonal voice, drawing on examples from the children's work where possible.

Lesson 7

Spotlight on: Familiarisation

Teaching Objectives

- *To appraise a text quickly and effectively; to retrieve information from it; to find information quickly and evaluate its value (Y6 T3 T17)*
- *To select the appropriate style and form to suit a specific purpose and audience, drawing on knowledge of different non-fiction text types (Y6 T3 T22)*

Whole Class Shared Reading

Work through the book looking at, and listing, all the ways that information is presented, e.g. text, photographs, diagrams, charts.

Return to pages 10 and 11. Discuss with the children alternative ways of presenting the causes and effects of global warming in a format that is easy to read at a glance. Allow this to be an open activity, encouraging children to make their own suggestions with as little prompting as possible.

Group Activities

In pairs, the children can re-present the explanation of global warming in the way that they feel would be most effective.

Plenary

Ask the children to present their explanations and to explain why they chose that format.

Display effective examples along with the children's rationales.

Lesson 8

Spotlight on: The writing process

Teaching Objectives

- *To select the appropriate style and form to suit a specific purpose and audience, drawing on knowledge of different non-fiction text types (Y6 T3 T22)*
- *To revise the language conventions and grammatical features of the different types of text (Y6 T3 S1)*
- *To secure control of complex sentences, understanding how clauses can be manipulated to achieve different effects (Y6 T3 S4)*

Whole Class Shared Writing

Explain to the children that as a class they are going to plan, write and publish a quiz book on the subject you identified at the beginning of this unit.

Discuss a potential audience and the purpose of quizzes. You may wish to show examples of quizzes and quiz books e.g. 'What am I?' or True or False? books, and quizzes in magazines.

Decide how the quiz will work and what form it will take, e.g. answers written upside down, on the next page, hidden under flaps, at the back of the book. Discuss the suitability of the children's suggestions.

Ask the children to suggest questions for the book. List these.

Take one of the questions and, with the children, plan and draft the answer in the form of an explanation. Discuss the need for an extended answer in order to broaden the reader's knowledge.

Allocate questions to pairs, individuals or groups.

Group Activities

The children can plan and draft their answers as explanations. Some children may need the support of the explanation framework on PCM 1 (see page 56).

Plenary

Discuss whether any of the children feel that an illustration of some kind is necessary to support their explanation.

Ask the children to indicate in their drafts the kind of illustration they would add, e.g. map, diagram, flow chart.

Lesson 9

Spotlight on: The writing process

Teaching Objectives

- *To revise the language conventions and grammatical features of the different types of text (Y6 T3 S1)*
- *To revise formal styles of writing (Y6 T3 S3)*

Whole Class Shared Writing

Return to the draft explanation. Is an illustration necessary? Where should it go?

Edit the draft. Focus on typical language features, e.g. cause and effect connectives, impersonal voice.

Group Activities

The children can edit their drafts and, where necessary, plan their illustrations.

Plenary

The children can read their questions and answers to the rest of the class. Encourage others to make constructive criticisms about the clarity of the explanations.

Lesson 10

Spotlight on: The writing process

Teaching Objectives

- *To revise the language conventions and grammatical features of the different types of text (Y6 T3 S1)*
- *To revise formal styles of writing (Y6 T3 S3)*

Whole Class Shared Writing

Discuss with the children how the quiz book will be compiled and published.

Allocate roles and identify a time when the final stages will be completed.

Group Activities

The children can bring their work to publication standard and add illustrations.

Plenary

Review the features of explanations and discuss the purposes of the text type.

Ask the children to think about when they have written or read explanations in other subjects and outside the school environment.

Name

Explanation framework

<u>Statement about phenomenon</u>

<u>Sequenced explanation</u>

<u>Concluding or summary statement</u>

Text type: Explanation (*Quakes, Floods and Other Disasters*)
Links with Literacy Lesson: **Year 6, Unit 4, Lessons 1 and 8**

Name

Name that text

Here are four pieces of writing about polar bears.
What is the text type of each piece of writing?

1 In order to track and observe the polar bear in its natural habitat, it is important to remember the following points: wear appropriate clothing; keep a safe distance between yourself and the bear; stay downwind; avoid any sudden movements.

If you follow these points, your tracking will be an enjoyable experience for you and non-threatening for the bear.

2 In recent years, hunters have been responsible for a dramatic decline in the polar bear population. We need to take action before the polar bear becomes extinct.

Polar bears are an important part of the wildlife of the Arctic region. Without them preying on other animals, such as walruses and seals, these animals would increase in numbers and the balance of nature would be disturbed.

Without polar bears, our planet would have lost one of its most interesting and attractive mammals.

3 The polar bear is a large, white bear that lives in Arctic regions. The bear is between 1.8 and 2.4 metres long and can weigh up to 770 kg.

The polar bear feeds mainly on walruses and seals, although during the summer it will sometimes eat berries, birds' eggs and other food.

The female polar bear produces her cubs in winter. She stays with them in a snow cave until spring, feeding them herself. Once there were many thousands of polar bears, but over-hunting drastically reduced their numbers.

4 The polar bear is found in Arctic regions and has a number of distinctive features.

In the cold Arctic, the bear needs to keep warm. To help this, its skin is black. Because dark colours absorb heat, this means that the bear's skin is able to trap heat from the sun.

Two other features help the bear move easily in its environment. Furry soles on its feet help it to move safely over smooth ice and a membrane between its toes helps it to swim.

The polar bear is a protected animal, but may be hunted by local people or for scientific research.

Text type: Explanation (*Quakes, Floods and Other Disasters*)
Links with Literacy Lesson: **Year 6, Unit 4, Lesson 1**

PCM

Active to passive

Turn these active sentences into passive sentences, then try to delete as many words as possible while still retaining the meaning of the sentence. The first one has been done for you.

1 High winds wrecked Mr Jones' garage.
  ~~Mr Jones'~~ garage ~~was~~ wrecked ~~by high winds~~.
  Garage wrecked.

2 Lack of rain causes water shortage.

3 A gang vandalised the playground.

4 The governors gave St James' school an extra day's holiday.

5 Judges praised Meera for her excellent singing.

6 The children collected eight bags of toys for the local hospital.

7 Hygiene inspectors closed the local fish and chip shop.

8 Animal rights campaigners release mink into the wild.

9 Too many cattle are eating the grass.

10 100 acres of forest were destroyed in the fire.

Text type: Explanation (*Quakes, Floods and Other Disasters*)
Links with Literacy Lesson: **Year 6, Unit 4, Lesson 2**

© Reed Educational and Professional Publishing Ltd, 1999

Name

Persuasion framework

Background information or issue

Statement of point of view

Facts or information with evidence

Conclusion

Text type: Explanation (*Quakes, Floods and Other Disasters*)
Links with Literacy Lesson: **Year 6, Unit 4, Lesson 5**

PCM **4**

© *Reed Educational and Professional Publishing Ltd, 1999*

Year 6: Unit 5

Reference: *An Encylopedia of Myths and Legends*

Introduction

Reference, or alphabetically ordered, texts feature in the range statements in the NLS *Framework for teaching* every year from Year 1. Prior to Years 5 and 6, children will have learned how to locate words by initial letter in alphabetically organised texts. They may also have made class dictionaries, glossaries or special interest encyclopedias.

Encyclopedias can vary in content, organisation and presentation. They range from the conventional, alphabetically organised multiple volume, e.g. *Children's Britannica*, to the single volume, subject specific, e.g. *Children's Encyclopedia of Science*.

All encyclopedias give concise information. *An Encyclopedia of Myths and Legends* gives information, in particular, about the gods, goddesses and characters in Greek, Roman and Celtic mythology. It can therefore be used to support historical studies in the curriculum.

Each entry in *An Encyclopedia of Myths and Legends* is organised in the same way:

Page headings
You can tell which letters are on which page by looking at the page headings. They show the first two letters of the first and last entries on each page.

Headwords
The headwords are the words being described in the encyclopedia. These are in **bold** type.

Pronunciation guides
The pronunciation of the headword, if it is particularly difficult or unexpected, is given in square brackets, e.g. [**back**-us]. The letters in **bold** show which syllable is stressed.

Icons
Each headword is followed by an icon, which tells you, at a glance, if an entry is about something Greek, Roman or Celtic.

Cross-references
Words used in the explanations may be explained somewhere else in the encyclopedia. If this is the case, the word will be in *italic* type. You can look it up to find out what it means.

Unit 5

An Encyclopedia of Myths and Legends

Text type: Reference

Learning Outcomes:

To become familiar with the content, structure and organisation of encyclopedias, and to learn to write an encyclopedia.

Preparation:

Collect a variety of encyclopedias, both general and subject specific. It would also be helpful to have a range of dictionaries and thesauruses and a selection of books containing puns and riddles.

Show the class the book you are going to study. Explain that you are going to work with a big book version of *An Encyclopedia of Myths and Legends* to ensure that everyone can see clearly.

Lesson ❶

Spotlight on: Immersion

Teaching Objective

- *To review a range of non-fiction text types and their characteristics (Y6 T3 T19)*

Whole Class Shared Reading

Show the children the cover of the *Encyclopedia of Myths and Legends* big book. Read the back cover blurb.

Discuss where in the book you could look to find further information on the content.

Read the introduction on pages 4 and 5.

Ask the children what entries they would expect to find in the encyclopedia. List their responses. Use the index to look these up.

Focus on the word *encyclopedia* on the front cover. Ask the children to look at other encyclopedia titles, and ask what they notice about the spelling of the word *encyclopedia*. Discuss why the spelling varies.

Group Activities

The children can complete PCM 1 (see page 63).

Plenary

Discuss the children's annotations and remind them of any omitted features and conventions. Draw the children's attention to subject specific encyclopedias, e.g. *Encyclopedia of Myths and Legends*, and general encyclopedias, e.g. *Encyclopedia Britannica*.

Lesson ❷

Spotlight on: Discovery

Teaching Objectives

- *To conduct detailed language investigations through interviews, research and reading (Y6 T3 S2)*
- *To practise and extend vocabulary (Y6 T3 W6)*

Whole Class Shared Reading

Write up the word *titanic*. Read the entry for *Titans*.

Ask the children what they think the word *titanic* means.

With the children, write a definition of the word, e.g. 'very strong, large or powerful'.

Write up the word *narcissistic*. Read the entry for *Narcissus*.

Ask the children what they think the word *narcissistic* might mean. Following discussion, write a definition with the children, e.g. 'to be obsessively interested in your own appearance'.

Group Activities

- Some children could confirm the class definitions of *titanic* and *narcissistic* by looking up and noting down the dictionary definitions.

  In pairs, children can list synonyms for the two words. Some children may need to use a thesaurus.
- The children could complete PCM 2 (see page 64).

Plenary

Ask the children to read out the dictionary definitions for *titanic* and *narcissistic*.

Compare these definitions to the class definitions.

Ask a few children to read their lists of synonyms. You may wish to list these. Discuss their accuracy.

Lesson ③

Spotlight on: Familiarisation

Teaching Objective

- *To practise and extend vocabulary (Y6 T3 W6)*

Whole Class Shared Reading

Mask the answer to the riddle under the entry for *Sphinx* in the big book.

Discuss riddles with the children, identifying what they are.

Ask the children to suggest answers to the riddle. Reveal the answer in the book and discuss its meaning.

Ask the children whether they know the answer to the riddle 'What is black, white and read all over?' (Answer – a newspaper).

Discuss the pun on the word 'read'. Talk about puns, explaining that they are a form of word play. Ensure that all children understand this term.

Group Activities

Ask the children to write down riddles and puns that they already know.

Plenary

Some children can challenge the rest of the class with their riddles.

Lesson ④

Spotlight on: The writing process

Teaching Objectives

- *To select the appropriate style and form to suit a specific purpose and audience, drawing on knowledge of different non-fiction text types (Y6 T3 T22)*
- *To conduct detailed language investigations through interviews, research and reading (Y6 T3 S2)*
- *To practise and extend vocabulary (Y6 T3 W6)*
- *To experiment with language (Y6 T3 W7)*

Whole Class Shared Writing

Explain to the children that they are going to produce a class book about playing with words. It could include puns, riddles, new or invented words and sayings that include figurative language, e.g. 'he split his sides with laughter'.

Identify an audience for the book.

Discuss how the book will be organised, e.g. alphabetically, thematically.

With the children, discuss and write up examples of the various types of word play that are to be included.

Group Activities

- Ask the children to plan and draft their entries for the class book. Encourage them to think about page layout, e.g. Will the answer to a riddle appear on the same page, at the back of the book, on the next page, upside down? Should illustrations be included?
- Some children could interview other children, members of staff, etc. to find further examples of word play.

Plenary

With the children, evaluate the content of the entries for the book. Discuss the suitability of entries for the intended audience.

Lesson ⑤

Spotlight on: The writing process

Teaching Objectives

- *To select the appropriate style and form to suit a specific purpose and audience, drawing on knowledge of different non-fiction text types (Y6 T3 T22)*
- *To conduct detailed language investigations through interviews, research and reading (Y6 T3 S2)*
- *To practise and extend vocabulary (Y6 T3 W6)*
- *To experiment with language (Y6 T3 W7)*

Whole Class Shared Writing

Discuss and decide upon a common page layout for the class book.

Display the plan or design so that children can refer to it whilst writing.

Identify any organisational and structural features that will be included in the book, e.g. contents, index. List these.

Group Activities

Ask the children to complete the writing of their entries for the book. These could be typed on the computer.

The book could be compiled either during this lesson or outside the Literacy Hour.

Plenary

If possible, use the book with the intended audience. Evaluate its success with the children and discuss any changes that they feel may need to be made.

Name

Features and print conventions of an encyclopedia

This is an entry from *An Encyclopedia of Myths and Legends*. Annotate the entry using these labels:

headword, italics,
cross reference,
colon, brackets,
icon, bold.

Bacchus [back-us] ℝ
(Dionysus **G**): god of festivities
and wine – which some say was
his invention. Bacchus' mother
died before his birth, but
Mercury (see *Hermes*) saved
him and sewed him into the
thigh of his father Jupiter (see
Zeus) from where he was later
born. He was so disliked by his
wife *Juno* that she drove him
mad. Afterwards he wandered
around the world with his wild
band of followers.

List some other features that are associated with encyclopedias.

Text type: Reference (*An Encyclopedia of Myths and Legends*)
Links with Literacy Lesson: **Year 6, Unit 5, Lesson 1**

PCM **1**

Name

What do they mean?

Phrase or word	Possible meaning
Achilles heel	
Herculean task	
Camelot	
Junoesque	
Cupid's arrow	
Pandora's box	
Holy grail	

Text type: Reference (*An Encyclopedia of Myths and Legends*)
Links with Literacy Lesson: **Year 6, Unit 5, Lesson 2**
Links with Guided Reading Card: **Stage 4, Card 9**

© *Reed Educational and Professional Publishing Ltd, 1999*

Year 6: Unit 6

Reference: *Roots and Routes: A Dictionary of Word Derivations*

Introduction

Reference, or alphabetically ordered, texts feature in the range statements in the NLS *Framework for teaching* every year from Year 1. Prior to Years 5 and 6, children will have learned how to locate words by initial letter and that dictionaries give definitions. They may also have made class dictionaries of special interest words.

Dictionaries may cover many subjects: idioms, slang, quotations, proverbs, slogans, as well as general dictionaries that focus on definitions of words. *Roots and Routes* explores words with interesting origins, giving a brief definition and an explanation of their derivations. The dictionary contains a full explanation of the way the entries are organised. Children should also be given the opportunity to explore other dictionaries.

Each entry in *Roots and Routes* is organised in the same way:

1. The headword is in **bold** type, e.g. **bloke**.

2. If the word is used informally (slang), this information is given immediately after the headword.

3. The part of speech is in ***bold italics***, e.g. ***noun***.

4. The word's meaning or meanings follow after the part of speech.

5. The period, century or date that the word was introduced in English is given, e.g. C19.

6. The language from which the word came, if known, is stated.

7. The original form of the word is shown in *italics*, e.g. *bloke*, and this is followed by the English translation in inverted commas, e.g. 'man'.

8. The entry may give further information on the route between the origin and the current meaning.

9. Cross-references are in SMALL CAPITALS.

10. Page headings are in **bold** type and show the first and the last entries on that page.

Unit 6

Roots and Routes: A Dictionary of Word Derivations

Text type: Reference

Learning Outcomes:

To understand the purpose and organisation of dictionaries; to explore word origins and to write and compile dictionary definitions.

Preparation:

Make a collection of dictionaries that serve various purposes, e.g. dictionaries of slang, quotations, proverbs, idioms, clichés.

Show the class the book you are going to study. Explain that you are going to work with a big book version of *Roots and Routes* to ensure that everyone can see clearly.

Lesson ❶

Spotlight on: Immersion

Teaching Objectives

- *To appraise a text quickly and effectively; to retrieve information from it; to find information quickly and evaluate its value (Y6 T3 T17)*
- *To practise and extend vocabulary (Y6 T3 W6)*

Whole Class Shared Reading

Show the children the cover of the *Roots and Routes* big book and discuss the title. What information do they expect this dictionary to contain? What helped them reach their conclusions?

Revise the function of an etymological dictionary and link this with the use of the words *roots* and *routes*.

Introduce and explain the term 'homophone'. Ask the children to suggest other pairs of words, and list their suggestions.

Read the introduction on pages 4 and 5 and '*How this dictionary works*' on page 8 of the big book.

Choose and read an entry, referring back to page 8 to ensure that children understand the organisation and features of this dictionary.

Write up the headings from PCM 1 (see page 68).

Demonstrate how to collect the data by filling in the information for *Roots and Routes*.

Explain that some dictionaries will also give other information e.g. pronunciation, plurals, participles.

Group Activities

- The children can review the dictionary collection and complete PCM 1 (see page 68).
- Some children can extend the list of homophones.

Plenary

Some children can report back on their reviews of the dictionaries.

Other children can give examples from their lists of homophones.

You may wish to start a class list of homophones which the children can add to from their reading.

Lesson ❷

Spotlight on: Discovery

Teaching Objective

- *To appraise a text quickly and effectively; to retrieve information from it; to find information quickly and evaluate its value (Y6 T3 T17)*

Whole Class Shared Reading

Look up and read the entry for *anthology*. Discuss the meaning and why an anthology might be referred to as a collection of flowers.

Focus on 'logia' Explain that it comes from *logos* meaning 'word' and that *-logy*, *-logist* and *-logic* are all endings derived from this Greek root.

Ask the children to suggest words with those endings, and list their suggestions.

Look up and read the entry for *chrysanthemum*. Explain that many words starting with *chr* have Greek roots.

Ask the children to suggest some words with this spelling pattern and list them.

Group Activities

Children can complete General PCM 3 (see page 72) using words from the list of *chr* words and others they can think of individually.

Plenary

Remind the children that knowledge of spelling patterns and derivations can help them work out spelling and meaning.

You may wish to start a class poster showing spelling patterns related to derivation and meaning.

Lesson ③

Spotlight on: Familiarisation

Teaching Objective

- *To use known spellings as a basis for spelling other words with similar patterns or related meanings (Y6 T3 W2)*

Whole Class Shared Reading

Look up and read the entries for *cursor, explode, focus, infantry, sinister* and *umbrella*.

Draw attention to the Latin root of each word and write these up.

Ask the children to think of other words that contain these roots e.g. *curs – cursive, cursory*. List these.

Discuss any patterns or related meanings in the list and how knowledge of meaning and spelling patterns can be an aid to working out meaning.

Write up the following words and explain that each has a Latin root: *statue, urban, August, square, author, oblong, favour, master, forum*.

Group Activities

The children can use etymological dictionaries to find the meaning and root of the words listed.

Plenary

Can the children think of any other words that contain the roots they have found?

You may wish to start a class poster of words that derive from Latin.

Lesson ④

Spotlight on: Familiarisation

Teaching Objective

- *To use known spellings as a basis for spelling other words with similar patterns or related meanings (Y6 T3 W2)*

Whole Class Shared Reading

Before the lesson, mask several meanings for the prefixes in Appendix 2, e.g. *omni-, manu-, mis-, trans-*.

Explain the function of prefixes and the fact that most derive from Greek and Latin.

Turn to Appendix 2. Focus on the prefixes whose meanings have been masked. Ask the children to suggest words that start with these prefixes and to give a definition for each word they suggest. List these.

Unmask the meanings of the prefixes and compare these with the children's suggestions.

Explain how knowing the meaning of a prefix is an aid to understanding the meaning of a whole word.

List the headings from PCM 2 (see page 70) and demonstrate how to complete the first entry.

Group Activities

The children can complete PCM 2.

Plenary

Some children can report back on how knowing the meaning of a prefix helped them work out the meaning of a word.

Lesson ⑤

Spotlight on: The writing process

Teaching Objectives

- *To select the appropriate style and form to suit a specific purpose and audience, drawing on knowledge of different non-fiction text types (Y6 T3 T22)*
- *To invent words using known roots, prefixes and suffixes (Y6 T3 W5)*
- *To experiment with language (Y6 T3 W7)*

Whole Class Shared Writing

Explain that the class is going to compile a dictionary of invented words.

Discuss and model how to build up an invented word. Select a root and add to it, e.g. *cursive*: 'malcursive', 'extracursive'.

Alternatively, you may wish to produce a dictionary of invented specialisms and specialists. Remind the children of the previous work done on *-ology*. Ask for suggestions for new types of specialist subjects e.g. *tuckology* – study of lunch boxes, *fizzology* – study of bubbles in drink.

Model writing an entry using standard dictionary conventions.

Group Activities

In pairs, the children can refer to posters and previous work to invent and define some new words.

Plenary

Some children can read aloud their new words and accompanying definitions.

Discuss the final format of the dictionary and any additional information it might contain.

You may wish to publish this as a big book or a new addition to the class collection of dictionaries.

Name _____

Dictionary review

Title	Publisher	Purpose	Information	Abbreviations	Other

 **PCM** **1**

Text type: Reference (*Roots and Routes*)
Links with Literacy Lesson: **Year 6, Unit 6, Lesson 1**

Name

Prefixes

Think of up to three words for each prefix. Try to use a dictionary
only to check meaning.

Prefix	Meaning and origin	Words	My definition	Dictionary definition
bi-		. . .	. . .	. . .
co-		. . .	. . .	. . .
ex-		. . .	. . .	. . .
extra-		. . .	. . .	. . .
micro-		. . .	. . .	. . .
mis-		. . .	. . .	. . .
mono-		. . .	. . .	. . .
multi-		. . .	. . .	. . .

Text type: Reference (*Roots and Routes*)
Links with Literacy Lesson: **Year 6, Unit 6, Lesson 4**

PCM **2**

© Reed Educational and Professional Publishing Ltd, 1999

69

Name _____

Keeping track of your research

Keep a note of the titles of the books you are using.
Use this grid to list useful pages or to make brief notes.

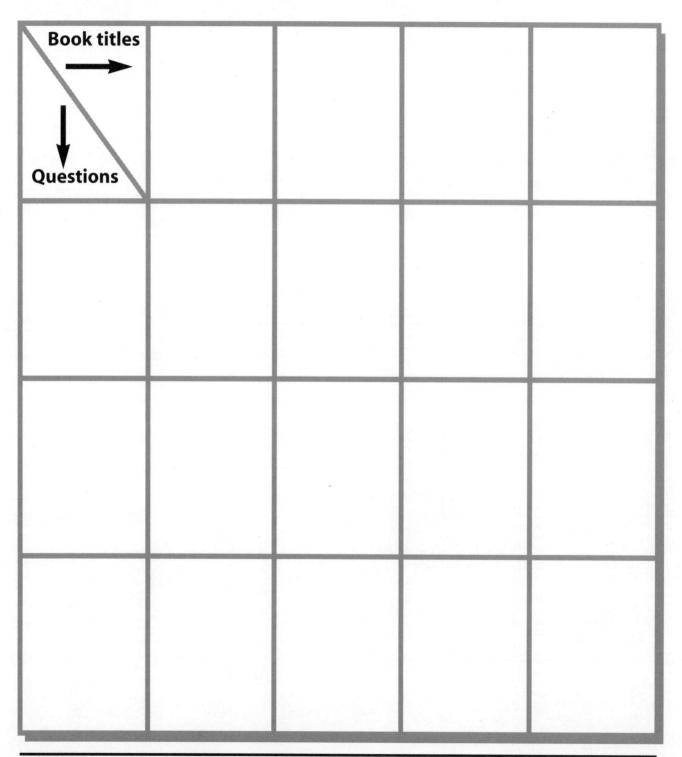

Book titles →

Questions ↓

GENERAL PCM

Text type: All
Links with Literacy Lesson: **Years 5 and 6**

Name

Read and reflect

Book title:

Author:

What I knew before reading this book

What I know after reading this book

Text type: All
Links with Literacy Lesson: **Years 5 and 6**
Links with Guided Reading Card: **Stage 4, Card 10**

GENERAL PCM

Name _____

What's in a word?

Dictionary definition	My definition	Word

GENERAL PCM 3

Text type: All
Links with Literacy Lesson: **Years 5 and 6**

Name

KWL chart

I already know

I would like to know

I have learned

Text type: All
Links with Literacy Lesson: **Years 5 and 6**

GENERAL PCM 4

Name

Non-fiction book review

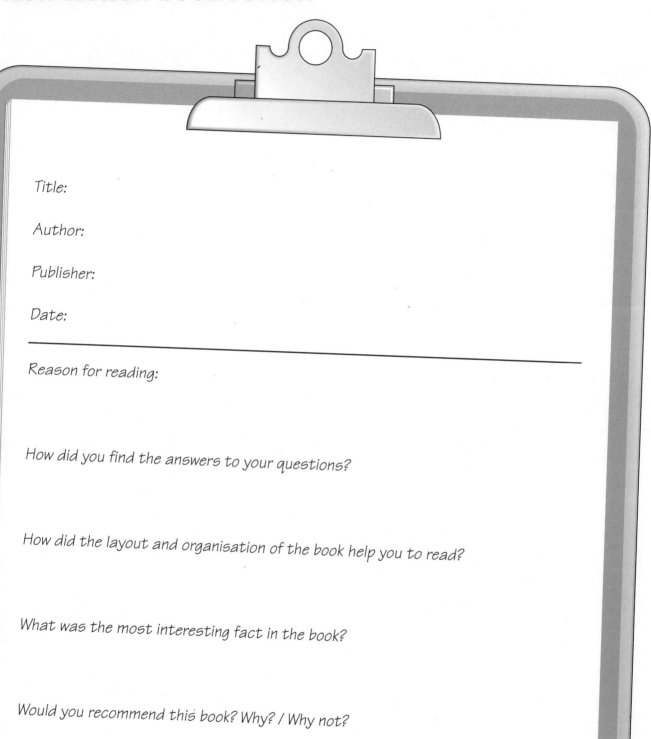

Title:

Author:

Publisher:

Date:

Reason for reading:

How did you find the answers to your questions?

How did the layout and organisation of the book help you to read?

What was the most interesting fact in the book?

Would you recommend this book? Why? / Why not?

GENERAL PCM ⑤

Text type: All
Links with Literacy Lesson: **Years 5 and 6**
Links with Guided Reading Card: **Stage 4, Card 4**

74

© Reed Educational and Professional Publishing Ltd, 1999

Name

Reading pictures

Look through the book and answer these questions.

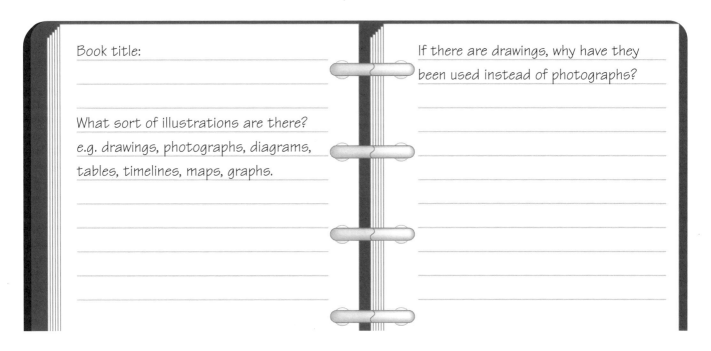

Book title:

What sort of illustrations are there?
e.g. drawings, photographs, diagrams,
tables, timelines, maps, graphs.

If there are drawings, why have they
been used instead of photographs?

Now choose a double page spread. Look carefully at the pictures
and read the text.

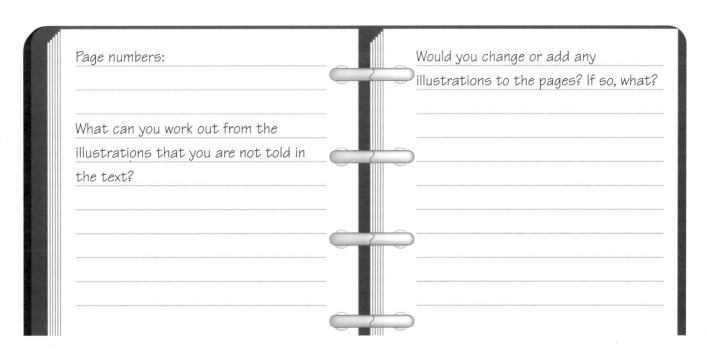

Page numbers:

What can you work out from the
illustrations that you are not told in
the text?

Would you change or add any
illustrations to the pages? If so, what?

Text type: All
Links with Literacy Lesson: **Years 5 and 6**

GENERAL PCM  **6**

Name

How I read non-fiction texts

Tick the boxes that describe what you do.

	Always	Sometimes	Never
I look at the cover and think about the content.	☐	☐	☐
I think about what I already know about the subject.	☐	☐	☐
I read from beginning to end.	☐	☐	☐
I flick through the book to get an idea of content and how the book is organised.	☐	☐	☐
I use the contents page to find out what the main sections are.	☐	☐	☐
I use the contents page to help me locate what I want to know.	☐	☐	☐
I use the index to help me locate what I want to know.	☐	☐	☐
I skim read a page and decide where to start reading.	☐	☐	☐
I read all the illustrations first.	☐	☐	☐
I read all the headings and sub-headings.	☐	☐	☐
I notice the different types of print e.g. bold and italics.	☐	☐	☐
When I want to locate a particular piece of information I scan the page looking for key words.	☐	☐	☐
When I find what I want on a page I read closely around the word to see if I can find out more.	☐	☐	☐
When I have finished reading, I think about what I have found out.	☐	☐	☐

GENERAL PCM ❼

Text type: All
Links with Literacy Lesson: **Years 5 and 6**

Name

How I write non-fiction texts

Tick the boxes that describe what you have done.

Date:

Title:

Text type:

In this piece of writing I have used:

Text

Title ☐

Main heading ☐

Sub-headings ☐

Paragraphs ☐

Captions ☐

Glossary ☐

Contents ☐

Index ☐

Grammar and punctuation

Full stops ☐

Commas ☐

Bullet points ☐

Bold ☐

Italics ☐

Process

Plan ☐

Draft ☐

Editing ☐

Proof reading ☐

Illustrations

Drawings ☐

Maps ☐

Plans ☐

Diagrams ☐

Graphs ☐

Photographs ☐

Time lines ☐

Boxes and arrows ☐

Language

Language features of ——————— text type

Technical words

Text type: All

Links with Literacy Lesson: **Years 5 and 6**

GENERAL PCM 8

Glossary

active voice   the use of active verbs to show the subject performs the action, e.g. *The dog bit Fred* (see **passive voice, voice**)

adjective   a word or series of words that describe or modify a noun or pronoun (see **comparative, superlative**)

adverb   a word or series of words that describe or modify a noun. Like adjectives, adverbs have three degrees of comparison: positive (the basic form), e.g. *soon, rapidly*; comparative: *sooner, more rapidly*; and superlative: *soonest, most rapidly*. Adverbs sometimes modify other adverbs or adjectives, e.g. *very rapidly, very beautiful*

argument   text where the emphasis is on persuading somebody to a point of view. It states a case or takes a position. Often several arguments are presented together (see **discussion**)

coherence   the connections in a text that make it logical and consistent

comparative   adjective indicating degree, more or less of a quality, usually formed by adding *−er*, e.g. *small + er*. With some longer adjectives *more* is used, e.g. *more beautiful*. Some adjectives have irregular comparatives, e.g. *little, less* (see **superlative**)

concept map or web   diagram used to organise and link ideas, information and concepts

connective   words and phrases that link a text together giving it **coherence**. Connectives vary according to the text type, e.g. **explanations** are linked through words like *because, this means that*; **arguments** are linked through *however, on the other hand*

cross-section   a diagram that reveals, in one plane, the inside appearance of a subject

cut-away   a diagram that 'slices off' part of the covering of an object to reveal what is inside it

discussion   text that presents more than one side of an issue; also called discursive text (see **argument**)

draft   early stage in the writing process; initial development of text from plan. Texts may be developed through several drafts. (see **revise, proof read**)

edit   the stage in the writing process where a text is reviewed and prepared for publication; attention is given to clarity and accuracy

ellipsis   **1.** the omission of a word or words needed to make sense, where the word is implied in context. Commonly occurs in speech, e.g. *'Have you seen Maggie since she came home?' 'Yes, on Tuesday.'* (*I saw her* implied). In writing, used for impact, to refine language and avoid repetition, e.g. *He gazed through the window and saw'* (*he* omitted)

2. a series of dots that indicate the omission of a word or words

explanation — text written to answer a question or explain a process

flow diagram or chart — a visual representation of information that uses lines, numbers or arrows to connect sequences or explain processes

font — technically, a variation in typeface, e.g. *italic*, **bold**: commonly used to refer to a family of type such as *Palatino, Times, Helvetica* (see **typography**)

genre — term often used to describe types of literary and non-literary texts, e.g. books, films; in educational contexts the term is used to describe different types of texts, written to achieve specific purposes (see **text type**)

gist — the main substance or essence of the text or matter being discussed or read

graphic design — the combination of visual and verbal elements to produce an integrated text; requires making decision about **layout, typography** and **signposts**

graphic outline — a diagrammatic representation showing how information is organised on a page (see **graphic design**)

icon — symbolic representation using pictures or images; often indicates an option or function, especially in computing

imprint page — page, usually at the front of a book, giving publishing information, e.g. *publisher's name and address, publication date, acknowledgements, printing details, ISBN*

information text — general description given to several non-fiction text types, i.e. those that inform (see **explanation, recount, report**)

instructional text — text written to tell the reader how to achieve a stated goal through a series of actions; sometimes known as a procedural text

key words — usually nouns and verbs, these words provide the key for understanding the main ideas in a text

layout — the positioning of visual and verbal elements on the page; includes the use of headings, paragraphs, arrangement in columns, placement of visual elements in relation to the text they illustrate

leaders, leader lines — lines or dotted lines drawn to link captions and illustrations, or items on the same line

non-chronological report — information text that classifies or describes, organised without reference to time

passive voice — the subject has the action done to it by someone or something else, who may or may not be identified, e.g. *Fred was bitten* (by the dog) (see **active voice, voice**)

person — a text may be written in the 1st, 2nd or 3rd person, i.e. *I, you* or *she/he/they*

proof read — to check writing prior to publication in order to find and correct errors

recount — a chronologically organised retelling of a past event or series of events

reference book   a source of information, typically arranged in alphabetical order, includes encyclopedias, dictionaries, gazetteers, also books with specific organisation such as atlases

report   non-chronological text written to classify and describe, may be about classes of things, e.g. *Dogs*, or describe one particular thing, e.g. *Our Dog*; usually written in the present tense; exceptions are reports that deal with historical subject matter

revise   stage in the writing process where the writer may add to, alter or restructure all or part of a draft

scan   look over a text quickly to locate specific information

signposts   features or devices use to organise and make links in a text and guide the reader; signposts include headings, sub-headings, cross-references, bullets, arrows, asterisks, **leader lines**

skim   read to gain a general impression of the subject matter, or the main ideas of a passage (see **gist**)

superlative   adjective indicating limit (most or least) of a quality, usually formed by adding –*est*, e.g. *small + est*. With some longer adjectives *most* is used, e.g. *most beautiful*. Some adjectives have irregular superlatives, e.g. *little, least* (see **comparative**)

synonym   a word which has a similar meaning to another

text type   terms used to describe texts which share a purpose, e.g. to recount, inform, instruct, persuade; each text type has specific features (see **genre**)

timeline   (see **flow diagram**)

typography   the design and choice of typeset material (see **font**)

visuals   the elements of a text that give information using few or no words; visuals include photographs, maps, diagrams, **timelines**, etc.

voice   refers to how the writer indicates the relationship between the subject of the writing and the actions associated with it (see **active voice, passive voice**)

writing frame   a prompt to support writing that reflects the structure and language typical of a particular text type, such as opening phrases for paragraphs